A COUNTRY DOCTOR'S
COMMONPLACE BOOK

A COUNTRY DOCTOR'S COMMONPLACE BOOK

Wonders & Absurdities

Very Best Wishes to
Brandon Gray.

Philip Rhys Evans

Philip

First published by Slightly Foxed in 2018

This collection and preface © Philip Rhys Evans 2018

Slightly Foxed Ltd
53 Hoxton Square
London N1 6PB

A CIP catalogue record for this book is available from the British Library.

ISBN 978-1-910898-14-7

Printed by Henry Ling Ltd, Dorchester

Preface

I had thought of keeping a commonplace book for many years. In my library at home I had gradually collected a few classic examples, such as Maurice Baring's *Have You Anything to Declare?*, John Murray's *A Gentleman Publisher's Commonplace Book* and in particular John Julius Norwich's annual *Christmas Cracker*. Finally, encouraged by my wife Christine and our three daughters, I sent out the first of my own small collections entitled *Wonders and Absurdities* to friends and family in time for Christmas 2002. *A Country Doctor's Commonplace Book* is a selection from this and fifteen that I have sent out each Christmas since. I am particularly grateful to *Slightly Foxed* for their enthusiasm in making it possible.

In 2002 I was still working as a GP in the lovely old market town of Bury St Edmunds. I arrived in Suffolk forty years ago after medical training at Guy's and spells as a GP in the wilds of New Zealand and Canada. In Bury I joined a practice of five doctors with a list of 10,500 patients, in both the town and nearly fifty villages scattered throughout the Lark Valley and neighbouring parishes. The practice had been established in 1902 and had adapted and evolved successfully through two world wars and the advent of the National Health Service.

One of its distinguishing features was its large number of loyal patients, some of whom had been born in the late nineteenth century. One, a very grand lady still living in her crumbling manor house at the age of 95, had been presented as a débutante to Queen Victoria in the last year of her reign. She and I became good friends and, once we'd dealt with the medical side of things, would enjoy swopping travellers' tales over a glass of sherry.

The practice of forty years ago was certainly a rather less hectic place than it is now. I remember a patient coming out of a consultation with one of the older partners and stopping at the reception desk to say, 'I think the doctor's gone to sleep.' In those early years I enjoyed the daily home visits to villages deep in the Suffolk countryside. If I couldn't find a patient's house or cottage, someone would inevitably appear from nowhere and point me in the right direction. Many of the older patients had known Dr Stiff, the founding partner of the practice, and I was only the fourth doctor they had had during their lifetime. In those days looking after four generations of the same family for more than thirty years was not unusual.

*

Over the years my own family – six brothers and sisters, six children, and a dozen grandchildren aged from 8 to 28 – have embraced the idea of the Commonplace Books, often telephoning, writing or now more usually emailing with a potential item. Happily for me some of them have settled abroad – an excuse for regular visits, particularly to Australia when it's their turn to host the Ashes.

Friends and acquaintances – many of them members of the Straw Boater Club, a dining club formed by a small group of medical friends which is now in its twenty-second year and has recently celebrated its hundredth meeting – are also keen contributors. In particular, thanks go to my sharp-eyed brother-in-law Neil Doherty and Jim Cox, my modest and understated Cumbrian correspondent. Absolutely indispensable to the operation are my wife Christine, now retired from managing a local legal practice, who supports, encourages and advises, and my secretary and good friend Rachel Harman, who with her advanced computer skills does the really hard work of putting the selection into comprehensible form ready for printing.

Newspaper cuttings and other contributions arrive out of the blue throughout the year and join the growing collection in the study.

There can be periods of steady flow, often followed by several weeks, even months, of drought. Then, suddenly and unexpectedly, items will start appearing again, often tumbling one after another like wickets in a cricket match.

Work begins in October, when Christine and I make a selection according to a set of unwritten and undisclosed criteria. The common threads are delight, surprise, wit, beauty, good sense and absurdity. Inevitably the selections reflect many of my own interests – history, wine, sport of all kinds but especially cricket, biography, novels, poetry, the writings of Chekhov and P. G. Wodehouse, obituaries of unusual and often eccentric individuals, letters to editors, travel, the Church of England as a spectator sport, and the bizarre oddities of British politics.

Life as a country GP exposes one to an extraordinary range of people and situations – always fascinating, sometimes absurd, often sad and poignant. I hope this small book catches something of that infinite variety.

Philip Rhys Evans
Suffolk, 2018

For Christine

There'll always be an England

The church will host an evening of fine dining, superb entertainment and gracious hostility.

Pot-luck supper on Sunday at 5 p.m., prayer and medication to follow.

The ladies of the church have cast off clothing of every kind. They may be seen in the basement on Friday afternoon.

This evening at 7 p.m. there will be a hymn sing in the park across from the church. Bring a blanket and come prepared to sin.

Low self-esteem support group will meet Thursday at 7 p.m., please use the back door.

From the newsletter of the parishes of the Lark Valley Benefice,
including the villages of Fornham All Saints, Fornham St Martin,
Fornham St Genevieve, Culford, West Stow, Wordwell,
Lackford, Timworth and Flempton-cum-Hengrave

Some of the best (actual) headlines of 2003:

Cracks found on Governor's daughter

Something went wrong in jet crash, expert says

Panda mating fails, veterinarian takes over

Miners refuse to work after death

War dims hope for peace

If strike isn't settled quickly, it may last a while

Cold wave linked to temperatures

Red tape holds up new bridges

Man struck by lightning faces battery charge

New study of obesity looks for larger test groups

Kids make nutritious snack

Typhoon rips through cemetery, hundreds dead

Marriage

It turns out not just to be a convenient social construct, but seems to be good for your health. A report suggests it halves the risk of Alzheimer's because the companionship is good for us as we reach middle age and beyond. This may surprise some long-suffering practitioners . . .

Observer, 3 August 2008

Thinking my wife's hearing was failing I asked my doctor's advice.

'Stand far away from the kitchen and call out, "What's for dinner?"' he suggested.

I started from the hall. No response. Tried from the sitting-room. Still no response. No response when I tried from the kitchen door, so I went in, tapped my wife on the shoulder and asked again.

'Are you deaf? I've told you three times,' she said.

Tim Burton, Wokingham,
letter to the *Sunday Times*, 29 August 2010

For sale
Full set of encyclopaedias. No longer required because partner knows absolutely everything! Offers.

Teignmouth News, 10 October 2002

Family medicine

Sir,
Looking for signs of stress in our children, we concluded that they were immune but carriers.

John Fender, letter to *The Times*, 22 January 2003

While signing repeat prescriptions, I could not help overhearing a lively exchange of ideas between two elderly ladies:

'I still have these hot sweats, I thought they would have finished by now; wonder if he will put me on HRT. You seem to have no more sweats, how come?'

'My husband died in August and the shock of that seems to have taken them away,' replied the other.

'I will go home and kill the bugger.'

Dr Jafrie, from 'Plain Tales',
GP, 26 September 2008

Fire and ice

Some say the world will end in fire,
Some say in ice.
From what I've tasted of desire
I hold with those who favor fire.
But if it had to perish twice
I think I know enough of hate
To say that for destruction ice
Is also great
And would suffice.

Robert Frost, 1920

*Inscription on Frost's tombstone in Old Bennington Cemetery,
Vermont*

'I had a lover's quarrel with the world'

Doctrinal niceties

In 2005 the Government proposed a controversial Bill that would outlaw religious jokes. One of the finest, from America:

I was in San Francisco one night, walking across the Golden Gate Bridge, when I saw a man about to jump.

I said, 'Don't jump.'

He said, 'Nobody loves me.'

I said, 'God loves you. Are you a Christian or a Jew?'

He said, 'A Christian.'

I said, 'Me, too. Protestant or Catholic?'

He said, 'Protestant.'

I said, 'Me, too. What denomination?'

He said, 'Baptist.'

I said, 'Me, too. Northern Baptist or Southern Baptist?'

He said, 'Northern Baptist.'

I said, 'Me, too. Northern Conservative Baptist or Northern Reformed Baptist?'

He said, 'Northern Conservative Baptist.'

I said, 'Me, too. Northern Conservative Baptist, Great Lakes Synod; or Northern Conservative Baptist, Eastern Seaboard Synod?'

He said, 'Northern Conservative Baptist, Great Lakes Synod.'

I said, 'Me, too. Northern Conservative Baptist, Great Lakes Synod, Council of 1879; or Northern Conservative Baptist, Great Lakes Synod, Council of 1912?'

He said, 'Northern Conservative Baptist, Great Lakes Synod, Council of 1912.'

I said, 'Die, heretic!' And I pushed him over.

Emo Philips, American comedian

Ward round

A poster seen in a maternity ward: 'The first three minutes of life are the most dangerous.'

Underneath someone had added: 'The last three can be pretty dodgy too.'

The Times, 5 November 2015

While waiting for an invasive procedure in the Urology Department at Harrogate Hospital, they played 'Bridge over Troubled Waters'.

Nigel Heptonstall, Harrogate,
letter to the *Guardian*, 22 October 2011

'I always tell my ladies, if you don't open your legs, you will never have a baby.'

My sister Barbara, while taking part in the
BBC series *The Seven Ages of Man* (1969)
on behalf of the National Childbirth Trust

Important new research

What scent drives men wild?
After years of intense research, we know the definitive answer.
It is bacon.

Tanya Sanchez, perfume expert,
Observer, 14 September 2008

Sir,
All items of clothing worn in hospital, including trousers, carry bacteria. The Health Secretary's decision to banish long-sleeved white coats from hospitals brings to mind work carried out by the Public Health Laboratory Service several years ago.

Researchers found that the least spread of bacteria from surgeons occurred if they were naked and lightly oiled.

Norman Simmons,
Emeritus Consultant in Microbiology,
letter to *The Times*, 19 September 2007

Unusual English words

Batterfang (verb): to attack with the fists or nails, to beat or claw and claw at. This delightfully descriptive word's origin is obscure, although it is thought to derive from Northern English dialect.

Dontopedalogy (noun): the science of opening your mouth and putting your foot in it. Prince Philip, Duke of Edinburgh, is credited with coining this word for his tendency to make faux pas.

Eximious (adjective): select, excellent

Kakistocracy (noun): the system of government in which the rulers are the least competent, least qualified or most unprincipled citizens

Limicolous (adjective): living in mud

Perjink (noun): a fusspot, an 'old maid'; (adjective): 1. neat, having a smart appearance, 2. prim, strait-laced, 3. exact, precise, scrupulously careful, fussy, finicky. Scots word.

Quisquous (adjective): perplexing, debatable, dubious

Teeter Totter (noun or verb): Norfolk for see-saw

Zoftig (adjective): 1. Full-bosomed, 2. having a full shapely figure, buxom. The word is derived from the Yiddish *zaftik* – juicy.

What's in a name?

When visiting friends in Perthshire, I have often driven through the village of Dull. I was refreshed last year to note that Dull is now twinned with the town of Boring, Oregon, and was further cheered the other day to see that there has been an approach from Bland in New Zealand, to ask if it can be twinned with both of them.

From Mark Conroy

Dear Sir,
The letters on amusing village names remind me of my favourite graffito. In south Lincolnshire, under the signpost 'To Mavis Enderby and Old Bolinbroke' someone had added 'The gift of a son'.

From Neil Noble

The Client Service Manager for F&C Fund Management Ltd is a Mr Phil Turnpenny.
The Spokesman for the Cumbria Ambulance Service is a Mr Rick Shaw.
Doctors Boyle and Burnham are in practice in Puddletown.
Natural England's Species Officer in Truro is Dr Jane Squirrel.
The Senior Customer Services Manager at the Leamington Spa branch of the HSBC Bank is Mr Nick Cashmore.
The Council for Science and Technology boasts among its members Dr Sue Ion.
I am reminded that the owner of the garage where my father used to leave his car on holidays in Cornwall was Mr Basher.
And perhaps the best of all . . . A previous Keeper of the Fabric at Westminster Abbey was Mr Buttress.

From assorted newspapers

Off the rails

Lal Bihari, a man in Uttar Pradesh, India, applied for a bank loan in 1976. When refused he found he had been officially declared dead by the authorities. He proceeded to fight an 18-year legal battle in an attempt to prove he was in fact still alive.

During this time he organized his own funeral, demanded widow's compensation for his wife and even went as far as standing for Prime Ministerial election against Rajiv Gandhi in his attempt to prove he was in fact still alive and kicking.

He founded the 'Association of Dead People' which ironically has a recorded 20,000 members throughout India. Finally in 2004 he managed to have his official death annulled, making himself ineligible as a member of his own Association.

Thanks to my daughter Suzanne, who heard it
on the radio but can't remember when

On one occasion when it was reported to a Congress leadership meeting that it was proving difficult to book an entire third-class railway compartment for Gandhi and his entourage, Sarojini Naidu snapped at him: 'It is becoming increasingly costly for us to keep you in the poverty to which you've become accustomed.'

Tariq Ali, book review,
London Review of Books, 8 July 2004

The letters about travelling on Indian railways . . . brought to mind the following story told to me by a friend. The train for his destination duly arrived, but when he got on he found his seat, which he had reserved, was occupied by a Sikh gentleman. My friend checked the carriage and seat number and found them to be correct, so asked the man to move. He showed him his reservation, with the carriage and seat written on it, saying: 'Surely you must agree that you are sitting in my place?'

'It is true that I am sitting in that seat,' said the man, 'but this is yesterday's train.'

Peter Crawley, letter to the *Independent*, 1989

What Britain's rail network really needs

A train journey offers degrees of companionship to suit all. Contrary to popular belief, it is extremely rare to be trapped with a bore, unless of course you married it and it bought the adjoining ticket. Never mind, by the time you pull out of Reading, you will have resolved to make neither of those mistakes again. Natural conversationalists seek each other out by means of cheery exclamations over dropped coffee lids and compliments about their temporary neighbour's children, handbag or packed lunch.

The naturally reticent gladly swap seats so that by the time the trolley arrives (which creates exactly the level of excitement at which the British psyche best operates), everyone is surrounded by the type of company most congenial to them. Would that all of life could be so sweetly and swiftly arranged.

The rail network does not need a massive overhaul, just a bit of tweaking to highlight its true attractions. Instead of spending billions on a new infrastructure, I suggest forking out £10.50 on a new set of stickers so that from now on we cannot just have 'quiet carriages' banning mobile phones but 'reading carriages' that proscribe all electronic devices, non-bookish children and noisy eaters, and a further £17 on furnishing 'reverie carriages' with little pillows to cushion heads that wish to rest against windows while daydreams dance within. Plus a few pounds on the self-explanatory 'kitten carriages' – why not! And a little more on oak panelling for 'Brief Encounter carriages' in which a willingness to embark on an unconsummated but terribly affecting affair can be signalled by wearing an ill-advised hat and sitting up straight. Now *that's* money well spent.

Lucy Mangan, *Guardian*, 15 August 2009

Grounds for complaint

A Yorkshireman had arranged for his wife's headstone to be prepared with a biblical reference. When he went to check the headstone, it said 'God she was thin'. He was upset at this and saw the stonemason and said 'You have missed out an "e".' The stonemason agreed that he would put it right. When the Yorkshireman went back to check the gravestone, it now said 'Ee, God she was thin'.

Letter to the *Guardian*, 31 January 2009

Sebergham churchyard is presently being cut by a contractor. Those who do not wish their graves to be cut are requested to let us know as soon as possible.

The Caldbeck, Sebergham & Castle Sowerby parish magazine (thanks to Jim Cox)

From a Methodist chapel noticeboard in Yorkshire:

'Christ was here.'

Somebody had scribbled underneath:

'Only if he knew that you had to change at Darlington.'

Thanks to John Horder

A really stiff drink

Sir,
Your report yesterday about that noble beverage, the Bloody
Mary, reminded me of a Russian recipe. It involves two minor
amendments to the standard formula. (1) For vodka, substitute
95% neat spirit, and (2) forget the tomato juice.

Mike Shotton, letter to The Times, 22 January 2002

The use of rubbish in contemporary art continues to confuse,
according to a report in the new issue of *Art Review*. The New
York artist Tony Matelli recently exhibited a sculpture of a semi-
naked woman surrounded by empty beer bottles and cans at an
Islington gallery. Unfortunately, the overzealous cleaners
removed the cans from the work, called 'Ideal Woman', on a
nightly basis. Even when a notice was put up making it clear
that the cans were art, it made no difference, still they were
swept away, forcing the gallery attendants to begin their day
knocking back the hard stuff so they could replace the empties.

Independent, 6 March 2002

On the boycott of French wines in America following the war in Iraq:

Exactly one week before a formal dinner at the American
Embassy in Paris attended by leading Bordeaux wine producers,
the Ambassador was asked whether he intended to divest the
embassy cellar of its French wines. 'Certainly,' he said, 'bottle by
bottle.'

Jancis Robinson, 'Corked', Financial Times, 26 April 2003

Flights of fancy

I am grateful to my secretary Rachel for discovering this on a website called 'Fun Stuff':

After every flight, Qantas pilots fill out a form, called a 'gripe sheet', which tells mechanics about problems with the aircraft. The mechanics correct the problems and document their repairs on the form, and then pilots review the gripe sheets before the next flight. Here are some actual maintenance complaints submitted by Qantas pilots (marked with a P) and the solutions recorded (marked with an S) by the maintenance engineers. By the way, Qantas is the only major airline that has never, ever, had an accident.

P: Left inside main tire almost needs replacement
S: Almost replaced left inside main tire

P: Test flight OK, except auto-land very rough
S: Auto-land not installed on this aircraft

P: Something loose in cockpit
S: Something tightened in cockpit

P: Autopilot in altitude-hold mode produces a 200-feet per minute descent
S: Cannot reproduce problem on ground

P: Evidence of leak on right main landing gear
S: Evidence removed

P: DME volume unbelievably loud
S: DME volume set to more believable level

P: Friction locks cause throttle levers to stick
S: That's what friction locks are for

P: IFF inoperative in OFF mode
S: IFF always inoperative in OFF mode

P: Suspected crack in windshield
S: Suspect you're right

P: No. 3 engine missing
S: Engine found on right wing after brief search

P: Aircraft handles funny
S: Aircraft warned to straighten up, fly right and be serious

Sign seen at a golf club in Scotland

Tips
1. Back straight, knees bent, feet shoulder-width apart
2. Form a loose grip
3. Keep your head down
4. Avoid a quick backswing
5. Stay out of the water
6. Try not to hit anyone
7. If you are taking too long, let others go ahead of you
8. Don't stand directly in front of others
9. Quiet please . . . while others are preparing
10. Don't take extra strokes

Well done, now flush the urinal, wash your hands, go outside and tee off.

Party tricks

At Oxford C. B. Fry's party trick was to leap backwards from carpet to mantelpiece from a standing fart.

Guardian, 1972, first edition

At Oxford C. B. Fry's party trick was to leap backwards from carpet to mantelpiece from a standing tart.

Guardian, 1972, second edition

At Oxford C. B. Fry's party trick was to leap backwards from carpet to mantelpiece from a standing start.

Guardian, 1972, third edition

Jim McGill, stunt man for Illinois Radio Station WQLZ, was entertaining the queue for a rock concert with his party piece – climbing on top of the station's outside broadcast van and firing rockets from his backside via a tube inserted in his rear end. Unfortunately, mid-show, there was a malfunction – a rocket exploded prematurely and Mr McGill was treated in hospital for burns to his launch pad.

Independent on Sunday, 16 May 2004

An unusual incident

Two British traffic patrol officers from North Berwick, east of
Edinburgh, were involved in an unusual incident while checking
for speeding motorists on the A1 Great North Road.

One of the officers used a hand-held radar device to check the
speed of a vehicle approaching over the crest of a hill, and was
surprised when the speed was recorded at over 300 m.p.h. The
machine then stopped working and the officers were not able to
reset it.

The radar had in fact locked on to a NATO Tornado fighter
jet over the North Sea, which was engaged in a low-flying
exercise over the Borders district. Back at police headquarters,
the Chief Constable fired off a stiff complaint to the RAF
Liaison Office.

Back came the reply in true laconic RAF style: 'Thank you
for your message which allows us to complete the file on this
incident. You may be interested to know that the tactical
computer in the Tornado had automatically locked on to your
"hostile radar equipment" and sent a jamming signal back to it.
Furthermore, the Sidewinder air-to-ground missile aboard the
fully-armed aircraft had also locked on to the target. Fortunately
the Dutch pilot flying the Tornado responded to the missile
status alert intelligently and was able to override the automatic
protection system before the missile was launched.'

Thanks to Fiona Dalziel

Good intentions go to pot

An elderly couple, a middle-aged couple and a young newly married couple all wanted to join the church. They were interviewed by the vicar, who said, 'We have special requirements for new parishioners. You must show that you can abstain from sex for a four-week period.' Each couple agreed and the vicar arranged to see them at the end of the four-week period.

The vicar went first to the elderly couple and asked, 'Were you able to abstain for the four weeks?' The old man said, 'No trouble at all vicar.' 'Congratulations. Welcome to the church.'

The vicar then went to the middle-aged couple and asked, 'Were you able to abstain?' The man responded, 'The first week was easy, the second more difficult, and I had to sleep on the couch for several nights in the final two weeks. But we managed it.' 'Congratulations, welcome to the church,' said the vicar.

The vicar went to the young newlyweds. 'Were you able to abstain?' The husband said sadly, 'I cannot tell a lie to get into the church. We were not able to go without sex for the full four weeks.' 'What happened?' said the vicar. 'Well,' said the young man, 'we were getting ready to decorate the front room and my wife bent down to pick up a pot of paint. When she bent over I was overcome with lust and took advantage of her right there.' 'I am very sorry,' said the vicar, 'but rules are rules. You are not welcome in the church.' 'I know,' said the young man sadly, 'and we are not very welcome in Homebase either.'

Thanks to Justin Allen

Nobody will ever win the battle of the sexes. There is too much fraternizing with the enemy.

Henry Kissinger

Signs of the times

Sir

Since we installed solar panels on our roof, the DAB radio switches off on the last of the hour pips, and the FM radio won't work if the sun shines.

Letter to the *Daily Telegraph*, 8 January 2014

Slouchers need apply

Beryl King, who owns two recruitment agencies in Hampshire, placed an ad with the local Job Centre that sought 'Warehouse packers who must be hard-working'. The ad was rejected because asking for 'hard-working' staff discriminates against those who are not.

Independent on Sunday, 22 August 2004

Sir,

I had a pair of chest waders – in my case chin waders, as I am somewhat short – that not only did not leak, but once saved my life. I was wading in the River Spey by Aberlour a few years ago when I stepped in a hole and lost my balance. I was swept away by the very fast current, and the waders filled with air, giving buoyancy. I floated about a mile downstream to the other bank, with rod and hat still intact. The ghillie on that beat hauled me out with a broad grin and a half bottle of whisky.

Letter to *The Times*, March 2016

Water-cooler moments

We shared water-cooler moments
Every other day
Wishful water-cooler moments
And they can't take them away
Wry, dry looks that had no witnesses
Rueful smiles and knowing grimaces
I can't prove it, but we shared them
And I like to think you cared then
That you weren't just being nice to me
You sent memos with your eyes to me
And I reciprocated
Though I may have mistranslated –
Meanings added, meanings missed –
I'm pretty sure I got the gist

We didn't ever action
Our un-minuted attraction
We each knew that we shouldn't
So we didn't, though we could, it
Seemed we had an understanding
Or that's how I understood it
Till that moment when you winced at me
Went halfway to convincing me
I'd passed the out-of-order line
And hovered on the borderline
Between being an embarrassment
And being charged with harassment
And then you merged with Marketing

And now to my intense regret
You use the little kitchenette
That's time-shared with the 2nd floor
A long mile down the corridor
The rest's not even history
There never was a you and me
Though there might have been so easily
There's a question that's implicit here
And I admit I'm begging it –
Okay, the word 'relationship'
Pudding-wise is over-egging it
But first stone-wise, let those who've never
Wished and wondered cast it –
It was a beautiful speculationship
While it lasted.

Matt Harvey

This is the excellent foppery of the world, that when we are sick in
fortune – often the surfeit of our own behaviour – we make guilty
of our disasters the sun, the moon, and the stars; as if they were
villains by necessity, fools by heavenly compulsion, knaves,
thieves, and treachers by spherical predominance, drunkards, liars,
and adulterers by an enforced obedience of planetary influence.

Shakespeare, *King Lear*

Speaking in tongues

Hindi, you see, is spare and beautiful. In it we can think thoughts that have the merit of simplicity and truth . . . English is not spare. But it is beautiful. It cannot be called truthful because its subtleties are infinite. It is the language of people who have probably earned their reputation for perfidy and hypocrisy because their language itself is so flexible.

Paul Scott, *The Jewel in the Crown* (1966)

American is the language in which people say what they mean, as Italian is the language in which they say what they feel. English is the language in which what a character means or feels has to be deduced from what he or she says, which may be quite the opposite.

John Mortimer

Since I started compiling my commonplace books I have resisted the temptation to include any quotes by George W. Bush, because in spite of there being amusing ones to relate, it all seemed far too easy. But in his final year as President, I relented.

At a conference discussing the importance of developing international business, he is quoted as saying: 'The trouble with the French is that they have no word for entrepreneur.'

An applicant for a job with the US Federal Government is filling out the application form. He comes to the question: 'Do you favour the overthrow of the United States by force, subversion or violence?'

After thinking about it, he ticks 'violence'.

Doug Fishburn, United States, letter to the *Guardian*

America, America!

Americans don't stand on ceremony. They make no distinction about a man's background, his parentage, his education. They say what they mean . . . they are irrepressibly good-humoured, ambitious and brimming with self-confidence in any company. Apart from that, I've got nothing against them.

Tom Stoppard, Dirty Linen & New-Found-Land (1976)

An epidemic of plagiarism at universities

Sir,
The story was often told of the American student who handed in an essay bought as being 'B' grade only to have it returned by his tutor with the comment: 'I am delighted to give this essay an "A"; I thought it deserved it when I wrote it 20 years ago.'

Ian Templeton, Edinburgh,
letter to The Times, 4 January 2016

Hugh Brogan discusses the religious revivals that took place in the American colonies in the mid-eighteenth century:

This sort of thing convinced tens of thousands that they must change their wicked ways; but, as in all such cases, a few years later, the effects had largely worn off and the good people of Boston and Philadelphia felt free to dance again. Many men of good sense, good nature or good education disliked its emotionalism and turned to Deism, Unitarianism or infidelity.

Hugh Brogan, The Penguin History of the USA (1985)

Anton Pavlovich Chekhov

Tolstoy's daughters are very nice. They adore their father and have a fanatic faith in him. That is a sure sign that Tolstoy is indeed a mighty moral force, for if he were insincere and not above reproach, the first to regard him sceptically would be his daughters, because daughters are shrewd creatures and you can't pull the wool over their eyes. You can fool a fiancée or mistress as much as you please, and in the eyes of a loving woman even a donkey may pass for a philosopher, but daughters are another matter.

Anton Chekhov

One may be awestruck by Tolstoy's mind, delighted by Pushkin's elegance, appreciate Dostoevsky's moral quest, Gogol's humour and so on. Chekhov, however, is the only man one would like to resemble.

Sergei Dovlatov, *Notebooks*

Pasternak described Chekhov's works as being like apples picked green from the tree, that keep on ripening and sweetening over time.

Henry Shukman, *Guardian*, 21 May 2005

Snoopers beware!

Sir,
Robert Crampton's article on bathroom cabinet snooping
reminded me of a friend who filled his bathroom cabinet with
table tennis balls when he had guests. He found it amusing to
see the snoopers' faces when eventually they emerged from the
bathroom after much clattering and after having spent a
significant amount of time repacking the shelves.

Letter to The Times, 1 May 2015

I take a version of a script down to Settle to be photocopied.
The man in charge of the machine watches the sheets come
through. 'Glancing at this,' he says, 'I see you dabble in play
writing.' Although this about sums it up, I find myself resenting
him for noticing what goes through his machine at all.
Photocopying is a job in which one is required to see and not
see, the delicacy demanded not different from that in medicine.
It's as if a nurse were to say, 'I see, watching you undress, that
your legs are nothing to write home about.'

Alan Bennett, diary, 16 February 1984,
Writing Home (1994)

A letter from the Inland Revenue

Dear Mr Addison

I am writing to you to express our thanks for your more than prompt reply to our latest communication, and also to answer some of the points you raise. I will address them, as ever, in order.

Firstly, I must take issue with your description of our last as a 'begging letter'. It might perhaps more properly be referred to as a 'tax demand'. This is how we at the Inland Revenue have always, for reasons of accuracy, traditionally referred to such documents.

Secondly, your frustration at our adding to the 'endless stream of crapulent whining and panhandling that vomits daily through the letterbox on to the doormat' has been noted. However, whilst I have naturally not seen the other letters to which you refer, I would cautiously suggest that their being from 'pauper councils, Lombardy banking houses and puissant gasmongerers' might indicate that your decision to 'file them next to the toilet in case of emergencies' is at best a little ill-advised.

In common with my own organization, it is unlikely that the senders of these letters do see you as a 'lackwit bumpkin' or, come to that, a 'sodding charity'. More likely they see you as a citizen of Great Britain, with a responsibility to contribute to the upkeep of the nation as a whole.

Which brings me to my next point. Whilst there may be some spirit of truth in your assertion that the taxes you pay 'go to shore up the canker-blighted, toppling folly that is the public services', a moment's rudimentary calculation ought to disabuse you of the notion that the government in any way expects you to 'stump up for the whole damned party' yourself. The estimates you provided for the Chancellor's disbursement of the funds levied by taxation, while colourful, are in fairness a little off the mark. Less than you seem to imagine is spent on 'junkets for Bunterish lickspittles' and 'dancing whores', whilst far more than you have accounted for is allocated to, for example, 'that box-ticking façade of a university system'.

A couple of technical points arising from direct queries:

The reason why we don't simply write 'Muggins' on the envelope has to do with the vagaries of the postal system.

You can rest assured that 'sucking the very marrows of those with nothing else to give' has never been considered as a practice because even if the Personal Allowance does not render it irrelevant, the sheer medical logistics involved would make it financially unviable.

I trust this has helped. In the meantime, whilst I would not in any way wish to influence your decision one way or the other, I ought to point out that even if you did choose to 'give the whole foul jamboree up and go and live in India' you would still owe us the money.

Please forward it by Friday.

Yours sincerely
H. J. Lee
Customer Relations

John Julius Norwich included this in his 2012 *Christmas Cracker*, with this explanation: 'The following letter from the Inland Revenue, passed on to me by Mark Tennant, was published in the *Guardian*, which had previously asked them for special, permission to print it'

,

Taxed with inaccuracy

HMRC has returned his tax return to a man in Evesham after he apparently answered one of the questions incorrectly.

In response to the question: 'Do you have anyone dependent on you?' the man wrote: '2.1 million illegal immigrants, 1.1 million crackheads, 4.4 million unemployable Jeremy Kyle scroungers, 900,000 criminals in over 85 prisons, plus 650 idiots in Parliament, and the whole of the European Commission.'

HMRC stated the response he gave was unacceptable. The man's response to HMRC was, 'Who did I miss out?'

Valley News [a monthly magazine which covers Wiltshire and North Dorset], January 2013

Proud to be British?

First, the good news: in a survey of how long men take to make love, British males beat all their international rivals by taking the longest to finish. Now the bad news: it was only 7 minutes 36 seconds.

But before the nation's women feel short-changed, they should spare a thought for their Turkish sisters. In Istanbul, men are finishing in less time than it takes to boil an egg.

The results of the survey, done by issuing couples with stop watches, are reported in the *Journal of Sexual Medicine*. They were: 1. Great Britain (7.6 minutes); 2. United States (7.0 minutes); 3. Spain (5.8 minutes); 4. Holland (5.1 minutes); 5. Turkey (3.7 minutes). There were no French or Italian contestants.

Dr Marcel Waldinger, of Utrecht University, said his team set out to measure 'intra-vaginal ejaculation latency time', which grown-up readers can work out for themselves. For the record, the shortest time was 30 seconds and the longest 44 minutes. His identity is a secret.

Independent on Sunday, May 2005

Thank you for your very helpful sex tips for the over-50s. I now look forward to an article on how to suck eggs.

Letter to the *Guardian*, August 2010

Keeping up appearances

'Careful grooming may take twenty years off a woman's age, but you can't fool a flight of stairs.'

Marlene Dietrich

It would be mortifying to the feelings of many ladies, could they be made to understand how little the heart of man is affected by what is costly and new in their attire.

Jane Austen, *Northanger Abbey*

'I used to be Snow-white, but I drifted.'

Mae West

Do it tomorrow; you've made enough mistakes today.

Dawn Powell

Anglo-Saxon attitudes

After he was exposed, Lambton told an Intelligence Officer that he had thrown himself into a 'frenzied' round of 'gardening and debauchery' to get over the fact that he had lost a three-year battle over the use of his father's title.

Washington Post, 2 January 2007

The man who originally recruited Chapman was a sort of Anglophile SS officer called Walter Thomas, who had Scottish ancestry. He went to Southampton University and, as a result of his wanderings around Britain before the war, he passionately believed that Morris dancing was the root of all culture; a theory that has never been repeated by anybody before or since. He actually, believe it or not, ended up teaching Morris dancing to the Wehrmacht.

Ben Macintyre, author of *Agent Zigzag*,
on the British double agent Eddie Chapman,
BBC Radio 4 *Book Club*, 3 January 2013

My father and he had one of those English friendships which begin by avoiding intimacies and eventually eliminate speech altogether.

Jorge Luis Borges

High spirits

Tessa Waugh's delightful tales of commuting bring back memories.

The exclusive W Club was for commuters on the 6.40 p.m. train from Waterloo to Winchester. We met in the restaurant car and ordered a whisky. We then had a chaser every time we went through a station beginning with a 'w' – Wimbledon, Walton, Weybridge, West Byfleet, Woking and Winchfield.

On arrival at Winchester we left our cars in the car park and phoned our wives to collect us.

C. J. Savoy, Hampshire,
letter to *Country Life*, 29 January 2014

During a reception for a South American country, the Foreign Secretary in Harold Wilson's government, George Brown, is rumoured to have approached an elegant figure in red silk and requested a dance. He was told, 'I refuse for three reasons: first, this is not a waltz but the national anthem; second, you are drunk; and third, I am the Cardinal Archbishop of Lima.'

Numerous sources online

Men from the Ministry

Sir Alan Campbell was head of chancery at the British Embassy in Paris under Christopher Soames in the late 1960s.

Of Soames, booming, hospitable and effective, he remarked, 'He was the reverse of an academic. Indeed, such educational establishments as he had attended left only a faint impression on his mind.'

Obituary, *Guardian*, 26 October 2007

As Foreign Secretary, Sir Alec Douglas-Home was determined to reduce the amount of paperwork.

One day a Private Secretary sent him a two-inch thick report on Icelandic Fisheries, with a note: 'The Secretary of State may care to read this over the weekend.'

Sir Alec returned it with his own note: 'A kindly thought, but erroneous.'

Richard Pearson

There'll always be an England (2)

Ladies, don't forget the rummage sale. It's a chance to get rid of all those things not worth keeping. Don't forget your husbands.

Don't let worry kill you, let the church help.

The men's group will meet at 6 p.m. Steak, mashed potatoes, beans and dessert will be served for a nominal feel.

From Yorkshire parish magazines
(thanks to Neil Walmsley)

Sir,
The correspondence on church facilities reminds me of a story I heard while living in Durham in the 1970s. An American tourist had approached a verger at the cathedral asking if there was a telephone she could use. 'A telephone?' came the outraged reply. 'It took us 800 years to get a lavatory.'

Letter to *The Times*, 19 December 2014

Our Local Newspaper Story of the Week Award goes
(and not a minute too soon) to the *East London Advertiser* for its
memorable:

Wapping Pensioner Wins Hollywood Oscar

'Sixty-year-old Helen Mirren, of Wapping High Street, scooped
the Best Actress accolade for her role playing The Queen,' the
paper helpfully explained.

Guardian, 6 March 2007

How to cook a salmon in a dishwasher

Season your salmon fillets and dot with butter, as you would if
you were going to bake them in the oven. Encase them in a
double layer of tinfoil and scrunch the edges together firmly at
the top. You don't want any holes. Place this parcel in an empty
dishwasher, on the top shelf. Don't add a dishwasher tablet!!!
Run the dishwasher on its longest and hottest setting. Avoid the
eco-friendly one, as the temperature won't get high enough to
cook the fish. When the dishwasher cycle is complete, remove
the salmon parcel, allow it to cool down a little, and then open
it. Check that the fillets are thoroughly cooked before tucking
in. This method works well for whole salmon too.

Country Life, 22 January 2014

Bibliomania

The custom of borrowing books confutes nature. In every other such situation, the borrower becomes a slave to the lender, the social weight of the debt so altering the balance of the relationship that a temporary acquisition turns into a permanent loss. This is certainly true with money. Yet it is not at all true with books. For some reason a book borrower feels that a book, once taken, is his own. This removes both memory and guilt from the transaction. Making matters worse, the lender believes it, too. To keep up appearances, he may solemnly extract an oath that the book be brought back as soon as possible; the borrower answering with matching solemnity that the Lord might seize his eyes were he to do otherwise. But it is all play. Once gone, the book is gone for ever. The lender, fearing rudeness, never asks for it again. The borrower never stoops to raise the subject.

Can book borrowers be thwarted? There are attempts. Some hopeful people glue stickers that read 'EX LIBRIS' to the inside covers (clever drawings of animals wearing glasses, adorable yet pointless, and the name of the owners): 'EX LIBRIS ROSENBLAT-TIMUS' – as if the presence of Latin and the imprint of a name were so formidable as to reverse a motor reflex. It never works . . .

There's no spectacle that is as terrifying as the sight of a guest in your house whom you catch staring at your books. It is not the judgemental possibility that is frightening . . . Indeed, most people would much prefer to see the guest first scan, then peer and turn away in boredom or disapproval. Alas, too often the eyes, dark with calculation, shift from title to title, as from floozie to floozie in an overheated dance hall. Nor is that the worst. It is when those eyes stop moving that the heart, too, stops.

The guest's body twitches; his hand floats up to where his eyes have led it. There is nothing to be done. You freeze. He smiles. You hear the question even as it forms: 'Would you mind if I borrowed this book?'

Mind? Why should I mind? The fact that I came upon that

book in a Paris bookstall in April 1969 – the 13th I believe it was, the afternoon, it was drizzling – that I found it after searching all year in North America for a copy; that it is dog-eared at passages that mean more to my life than my heartbeat; that the mere touch of its pages recalls to me a Proustian shower, my first love, my best dreams. Should I mind that you seek to take all that away? That I will undoubtedly never get it back? That even if you actually return it to me one day, I will be wizened, you cavalier, and the book spoiled utterly by your mishandling? *Mind?*

'Not at all. Hope you enjoy it.'

'Thanks. I'll bring it back next week.'

'No rush. Take your time.' [Liar.]

From *Bibliomania*, a one-man show written and performed by Roger Rosenblatt at New York's American Place Theatre in 1994

Let's buy a calendar for Arsène the Unready

Is there nothing that can be done to help football managers and players caught cruelly unawares by the start of the season?

If you have missed this voguish ailment doing the rounds, be assured it is something we should all take desperately seriously. Last week an outbreak was diagnosed when Celtic complained they were not ready to play Manchester United in their Champions' League match. Shortly before that, Arsène Wenger said it would take 10 weeks for his Arsenal Vincibles to be ready to embark properly on their various campaigns. Well, barely a week passes without José Mourinho explaining with a bitter shrug how unprepared Chelsea are for some tie or another.

Perhaps – and one is forced to think outside the box here naturally – the powers-that-be could expend more of their budget publishing the fixture list when it is drawn up, reminding clubs of the important part it will play in their next season, the better that managers are not so publicly embarrassed when they turn over a page in their diaries sometime in early October and discover that they have a Champions' League game pencilled in.

Every week sides who feel they really 'aren't ready' are pressurized by their peer group into taking the plunge. It's very much like losing one's virginity in the Mid-west.

Alas, whereas abstinence programmes have taken off in that forward-thinking region of the United States, there is no comparable support structure in the Premiership. And so it is that, for the next few weeks, Wenger will be condemned to live the football equivalent of that nightmare, when you find yourself shoved on to centre stage in a play and realize that you have completely forgotten to learn your lines.

It goes without saying this cannot be good for his notoriously fragile nerves. It is all very well warning him now that next season he may have to face Chelsea as early as the second half of August, and to plan his summer accordingly. Indeed, you could prepare him for the worst by hazarding that this might be the case every year for the rest of his time in English football. But as with the others who have been ambushed by the fixture list, this is not much use now, and our thoughts should be most compassionately with them.

Marina Hyde, *Guardian*, 21 September 2006

Sleeping partners

The bicentenary of the Cambridge Union was marked on Saturday with a debate that 'This house isn't what it used to be'. Baroness Mallalieu, the first woman to be president of the union, recalled her frisky days on the Backs during the summer of love. She then told a story about an octogenarian baroness holding court in a House of Lords tearoom. 'The trouble with being my age is that every man I have slept with is now dead,' this formidable woman declared. There was stony silence and then a shaky hand was raised by a man at the end of the table. 'Hang on, what about me?' he asked. The baroness reached for her glasses and stared at him before announcing: 'Sorry, I thought you were dead.'

Diary, The Times, 9 February 2015

14th August [2003]. Another death; Cedric Price, for many years the partner of Eleanor Bron and an inspirational figure to many architects. He was a figure of 18th century exuberance with views on conservation that were shockingly at variance with received wisdom. Cedric didn't believe in preserving buildings that had outlived their usefulness; he would have made a good character in a modern-day Ibsen play. At Cambridge as an undergraduate he was once in the Rex Cinema when the adverts came on, including one for Kellogg's Ricicles. 'Rice is nice,' went the jingle, 'but Ricicles are twicicles as nicicles,' whereupon Cedric boomed out: 'But testicles is besticles.'

Alan Bennett, Untold Stories (2006)

Eastern approaches

Last week the Defence Minister of the United Kingdom, Geoff Hoon, reportedly said in the Commons, 'Umm Qasr is a city similar to Swansea.'

It brought the following response from a British soldier patrolling Umm Qasr. 'He's either never been to Swansea or he has never been to Umm Qasr. There's no beer, no prostitutes and people are shooting at us. It's more like Neath.'

Sydney Morning Herald, 2003

When we anchored in Jeddah's outer harbour, the white town hung between the blazing sky and its reflection in the mirage which swept and rolled over the wide lagoon, then the heat of Arabia came out like a drawn sword and struck us speechless. It was a mid-October day 1916; and the noon sun had, like moonlight, put to sleep the colours. There were only lights and shadows, white houses and black gaps of streets: in front, the pallid lustre of the haze shimmering upon the inner harbour: behind, the dazzle of league after league of featureless sand, running up to an edge of low hills, faintly suggested in the far away mist of heat.

Opening lines of T. E. Lawrence's *Revolt in the Desert*, 1927

For the record

Our retelling of the story of The Man Who Never Was (News, last week) included several errors. The operation took place in 1943 not 1944; the Royal Navy took the body of Major Martin to a spot off the coast of Spain, not Sicily; the body was not dressed in Special Services clothing, rather the uniform of a supposed Major; the purpose of the deception was to convince the Germans (via the Spanish fascists) that the Allies were going to invade Greece rather than Sicily and had no connection to the following year's Normandy landings.

Observer, 18 May 2002

In our article about the adverse health effects of certain kinds of clothing, Pages 8 and 9, G2, August 5th, we omitted a decimal point when quoting a doctor on the optimum temperature of testicles. They should be 2.2 degrees Celsius below core body temperature, not 22 degrees lower.

In our interview with Sir Jack Haywood, the Chairman of Wolverhampton Wanderers, Page 20, Sport, August 11th, we mistakenly attributed to him the following comment: 'Our team was the worst in the First Division and I am sure it will be the worst in the Premier League.' Sir Jack had just declined the offer of a hot drink. What he actually said was: 'Our tea was the worst in the First Division and I am sure it will be the worst in the Premier League.'

Guardian, 16 August 2003

The sub-titles for the BBC's Ten O'clock News are produced live as the show is broadcast, which can lead to confusion or simply Freudian slips. As in the report on Yasser Arafat's death, during which it was announced that the UN had held 'a minute's violence' to commemorate his passing.

Private Eye, 26 November 2004

The pleasures of reading

What I set out to do was produce a library so wide-ranging that a person of reasonable education could stay here for two years and emerge quite happy.

The 11th Duke of Devonshire after he inherited
the title and moved into Chatsworth in 1950

Dispensary to the soul

Library inscription in Trajan's Forum, Rome

Typoglycaemia

Don't delete this because it looks weird. Believe it or not, you can read it.

I cdnuolt blveiee that I cluod aulacity uesdnatnrd what I was rdanieg. The phaonmneal pweor of the human mind

Aoccrdnig to rscheearch at Cmabrigde Uinervtisy, it deosn't mttaer inwaht order the ltteers in a word are, the only

iprmoatnt thing is that the frist and lsat ltteer be in the rghit pclae. The rset can be a taotl mses and you can still raed it

wouthit a porbelm. This is bcuseae the human mind deos not raed ervey lteter by istlef, but the word as a wlohe.

Amzanig huh? Yaeh and I awlyas thought slpeling was ipmorantt!!

MRC Cognition & Brain Sciences Unit, Cambridge

Edward Thomas

Over the land freckled with snow half-thawed
The speculating rooks at their nests cawed
And saw from elm-tops, delicate as flower of grass,
What we below could not see, Winter pass.

Edward Thomas, 'Thaw', 1916

Yes. I remember Adlestrop –
The name, because one afternoon
Of heat the express-train drew up there
Unwontedly. It was late June.

The steam hissed. Someone cleared his throat.
No one left and no one came
On the bare platform. What I saw
Was Adlestrop – only the name

And willows, willow-herb, and grass,
And meadowsweet, and haycocks dry,
No whit less still and lonely fair
Than the high cloudlets in the sky.

And for that minute a blackbird sang
Close by, and round him, mistier,
Farther and farther, all the birds
Of Oxfordshire and Gloucestershire.

Edward Thomas, 'Adlestrop', 1917

*Last year, quite unexpectedly, Christine and I found ourselves within
a mile of Adlestrop. We followed the signpost and drove into a small
village sheltered under a low hill. As we came to the village green,
acting as a backdrop to a bench was the large railway platform sign –
only the name.*

*Edward Thomas passed through Adlestrop in 1913 and wrote the
poem in 1917. Dr Beeching did for the railway in 1965.*

The Church of England

A small piece of constitutional history is being made this year and no one seems to have noticed. Before 2012 is out the 105th Archbishop of Canterbury will be named and, for the first time, the choice will be made entirely by the Church of England. Actually, in the great sweep of things, it's rather a big deal.

Since the Reformation, the post has been in the gift of the monarch – or in effect, in modern times, the prime minister. For nearly a millennium before that, the Pope had to approve the appointment and frequently said no. Think of all the blood spilt along the way: Thomas Becket murdered in the cathedral, Simon of Sudbury killed by the peasants, Thomas Cranmer incinerated by Bloody Mary, William Laud beheaded . . .

And now an obscure 16-member commission will sit down – probably it being the Church, over tea and biscuits with a small sherry to follow – and will name the successor to Rowan Williams, who resigned last week or, to put it another way, ran out screaming to the sanctuary of Cambridge University.

The recent history of this process is a delight for connoisseurs of British politics. Until the 1970s all bishoprics were in the gift of the prime minister. Some PMs couldn't care less, but Harold Macmillan revelled in it, partly because he was genuinely religious and partly because in the words of his biographer, D. R. Thorpe, 'he loved moving the pieces around the chess board'. It is said – and Dr Thorpe thinks it quite possible – that once Macmillan spent an entire morning puzzling out who should be made Bishop of Bath and Wells.

When the Church's biggest job of all became vacant, he was in clover. He decided to appoint Dr Michael Ramsey as the 100th Archbishop. No. 99, Geoffrey Fisher, was appalled. He told Macmillan, according to Dr Thorpe: 'Dr Ramsey is a theologian, a scholar and a man of prayer. Therefore he is entirely unsuitable. I have known him all my life. I was his headmaster at Repton.'

'You may have been his headmaster,' replied Macmillan, 'but you are not mine.'

In the 1970s Jim Callaghan gave away most of the power. Instead the Church nominated two candidates and the prime minister was able to choose between them. In 1990 the task fell to Margaret Thatcher who had been tormented throughout her reign by Archbishop Robert Runcie. The outstanding successor, it was widely agreed, would be Dr John Habgood, the Archbishop of York, who was regarded by Mrs Thatcher as another turbulent leftie. To ensure his victory, so the persistent story goes, the Church put up alongside him the most hopeless bishop they had. Thus it was that George Carey became Archbishop of Canterbury.

In 2007 Gordon Brown (where was his sense of fun?) decided this was a responsibility he could do without. The deal now is that two names will be put forward by the Church, a 'preferred candidate' and a 'second appointable candidate': an heir and a spare. The prime minister then commends the candidate to the Queen for her approval, although the formal election is left to the gloriously alliterative College of Canons of Canterbury Cathedral. The first choice has to get the job unless he sees sense and refuses to accept.

Does this rule out politics? Don't be silly. The chairman of the selection panel is chosen by the PM and the Downing Street appointments secretary is a non-voting member, so David Cameron will have two spies among the biscuits. However, 15 of the 16 voters come from within the Church and, if they are determined, no earthly or heavenly power can stop them.

It is, though, a very bizarre committee. Six of its members represent the Canterbury diocese, i.e. East Kent. Just one represents the worldwide Anglican communion, including such trivial places as the US and Africa. The main task of the new archbishop will be holding the global church together in the face of potential schism over women bishops and homosexuality, and trying to maintain the relevance of religion in an increasingly indifferent nation.

Anyway, mere Westminster politics is a vicarage tea party compared with clerical machinations. 'It's already decided,' claims one expert. 'It's Coventry.' The post is unofficially meant to alternate between the two wings of Anglicanism: the Anglo-Catholic Williams is supposed to be followed by an evangelical, and the Bishop of Coventry, Christopher Cocksworth, fits the bill.

Opinion is moving against the old stagers, the Archbishop of York, John Sentamu ('a self-publicist,' says another source), and the Bishop of London, the sonorous and impressive Richard Chartres, who is perceived as being a bit anti-women priests. Instead attention is moving towards the unsullied but obscure Mr Cocksworth, Graham James of Norwich ('nice but managerial') and Nick Bains of Bradford ('a classic trendy vicar').

All this is duly being reflected by the successors to the monks and scribes, the bookmakers. Does the Church mind this? 'Oh, no,' said a spokesman. 'But we do have a laugh about it, especially when they quote prices for people who have been retired for years. We do have a problem with excessive gambling, but we're not against a little flutter.'

You do have to love the Church of England, really you do.

Matthew Engel, *Financial Times*,
23 March 2012

There'll always be an England (3)

Irving Benson and Jessie Carter were married on October 24 in the church. So ends a friendship that began in their schooldays.

At the evening service tonight, the sermon topic will be 'What is Hell?' Come early and listen to our choir practice.

Eight new choir robes are currently needed due to the addition of several new members and to the deterioration of some of the older ones.

The pastor would appreciate it if the ladies of the Congregation would lend him their electric girdles for the pancake breakfast next Sunday.

From the newsletter of the parishes of the Lark Valley Benefice, including the villages of Fornham All Saints, Fornham St Martin, Fornham St Genevieve, Culford, West Stow, Wordwell, Lackford, Timworth and Flempton-cum-Hengrave

Another good thing about the Berliner format: the cellos, who we sit behind in our orchestra, are appreciating the decreased disturbance level caused by the smaller rustle when pages of the *Guardian* are turned during sections when we trumpets are not required. Unfortunately the sections requiring trumpets are as disturbing as ever.

Letter to the *Guardian*, December 2005

General Practice

I once told a woman patient that she could stop taking the tablets. She replied: 'Oh very good, doctor, thank you, doctor. I wouldn't want to continue being under the affluence of drugs.'

The old handwritten GP notes, in what were called Lloyd George envelopes, provided a temptation to doctors when patients left their list and moved to a new part of the country.

One GP, when a particularly troublesome patient moved away, always wrote *'Caveat emptor'* in large letters on their medical record envelope before forwarding it to the family doctor who had unwittingly taken them on.

Another, in similar circumstances, invariably made a last entry in their notes thus: *Hamlet*, Act 1, Scene 1, Line 7, Francisco to Bernardo, 'For this relief, much thanks.'

But, 'Hurrah, hurrah, she's going to Crewe' would perhaps say more about the patient's doctor than the patient.

Abstracted from letters to *The Times*, 1986

Sir,
My late father-in-law, a GP, finding himself threatened by a patient who disagreed with his assessment of their fitness to work, conceded by issuing a certificate. On it he recorded the reason for unfitness as 'disinclination'. It was never challenged.

Letter to the *Daily Telegraph*, 22 April 2003
(thanks to my sister Barbara)

And the Oscar will go to . . .

2012 *The Wulfman*: a triumphant return to form for Mel Gibson, directing himself in the role of Aethelwulf, King of Wessex from 839 to 858. Gibson presents a typically dark and savage portrait of a man who was traumatized by the diphthong at the start of his name, and generally scared of long vowels, which in those days could spring up and attack at any moment. Over time, he learns to place his trust in consonants, thanks to the wise counsel of a marauding Dane named Knt. Dialogue entirely in Anglo-Saxon. With subtitles.

2013 *House:* After *The Queen, Elizabeth*, and *The Young Victoria*, which British queens remain to be explored? Step forward Anne (played by a pitch-perfect Hugh Laurie), who reigned from 1702 to 1714, and who is now mainly associated with an elegant style of architecture and furniture. The last word in country-house period drama, with its soundtrack scored exclusively for cello, harp and panpipes, and a controversial winner over David Fincher's blistering, bang-up-to-date texting drama *Elimin 8*. With Sir Michael Gambon, as Blenheim Palace, and a brief but scene-stealing turn from Dame Judi Dench, as a wingback chair with cabriole legs.

2014 *The Sadness of King George:* What would Christopher Nolan, the young British master of spectacle, do next? How could he top the wizardry of *Batman Begins, Inception* and 2012's *The Dark Knight Rises*? Not to worry; both his fans and – at last – the Academy were blown away by this low-key study of either George I or George II. (In a neat Nolan touch, the movie stays tantalizingly unclear on the matter.) One of the duller British rulers, George (Jude Law) wasn't tortured with doubt, just slightly unhappy in the mornings, and the film shows the devoted attempts of Lord Jollify (Jim Broadbent) to cheer him up with a string of faintly risqué jokes. Every penny of the five-million-dollar budget is blazingly there on screen. The croquet match in the topiary is a standout, and Nolan's flair for visual effects is confirmed by the now famous scene in which the King whips off his powdered grey 'hair' to reveal that, all along, it has been a wig.

2017 *Six*: A bearded and belching Helen Mirren extends her extraordinary range with a dazzling portrayal of Henry VIII, in this gender-twisting take on the uxorious thug. In the same spirit, his wives are cast as follows: Catherine of Aragon (Ray Winstone), Anne Boleyn (Robbie Coltrane), Jane Seymour (Brendan Gleeson), Anne of Cleves (Gary Oldman), Catherine Howard (Timothy Spall) and Catherine Parr (Don Cheadle, reprising his spot-on Cockney accent from *Ocean's Eleven*). Plus a delicious cameo from Sir Colin Firth as Chopper, the black-hooded kind-hearted executioner who talks the burly sovereign through his deepest marital fears.

2018 *The Naked Hunch*: Not a re-release of *Richard III*, the Laurence Olivier classic, but a vivid new telling of the same tale, as the badly disabled monarch is helped to see past his affliction – not an easy thing to do when he's looking over his shoulder – with the assistance of the red-hot widow Lady Anne (Carey Mulligan). Hugh Grant revives his career in the lead role, throwing in a stammer for good measure. According to insiders, the Oscar was clinched by the tag-line on the poster, 'It's a Hump. Get Over It.'

Anthony Lane, *The New Yorker,* 14 March 2011

In vino veritas

Harold Macmillan was in conversation with Lord Carrington some time in 1972. Ed Muskie, a Democratic candidate for president, had apparently broken down and cried when a New Hampshire paper accused his wife of being a drunk. Though he insisted that the tears were actually melted snowflakes, the incident ruined his image as calm and measured, and he left the race.

'What an extraordinary reason,' said Macmillan.

'I don't know,' Carrington is said to have replied, 'what would you have said if a newspaper claimed that Lady Dorothy was an alcoholic?'

'I would say,' said Macmillan, 'you should have seen her mother.'

Simon Hoggart, Guardian, 14 May 2011

An old woman is sipping a glass of wine while sitting on the patio with her husband, and she says, 'I love you so much, I don't know how I could ever live without you.'

Her husband asks, 'Is that you or the wine talking?'

She replies, 'It's me, talking to the wine.'

Thanks to my daughter-in-law Sally Winter

Geoff Howells' suggestion that one should put a brick in the lavatory cistern to save water ('Getting the Builders In', 9 December 2004) reminded me of the severe drought we had in either the late '40s or early '50s, when the same suggestion was made. I did not have a brick, but I had just finished a bottle of Gordon's Gin. I realized that if I filled the bottle with water and replaced the cap, it would have nearly the same displacement as a brick. So I did.

Months later, I called in the plumber to deal with a leak somewhere in the cistern. Returning home in the evening, I found the gin bottle on the hall table. With the plumber's bill was a note which read: 'With respect, sir, I do not think a lavatory cistern is a suitable place for the storage of your alcohol supply. You have my sympathy and understanding, as my late mother was a secret drinker.'

Bill North, Leeds,
letter to *Country Life*, 27 January 2005

Transports of delight

The bus I got into at Piccadilly Circus was one of those which the London General Omnibus Company calls 'pirates'. These shabby buses are always slow starters, since they hope to pick up as many passengers as possible. At Trafalgar Square several people got in and then got out again, irritated by the dallying demeanour of the 'pirate'. I felt impatient myself, and was about to get out. Then I noticed the face of the conductor. He was a tired middle-aged man with a gentle diffident expression. I saw that he was sadly aware of his vehicle's lack of prestige. He stood – one hand on the bell string – with a patient humble look which made me sympathetic. So I remained where I was, meditating on the humanizing effect of the episode. And I was rewarded, for the old bus went down Whitehall at full gallop. I watched the grey-haired man gently collecting the pennies; he smiled charmingly at two poorly-dressed little boys, and I was glad to be healed by such simplicity. Strange that one can get a moral lesson from a motor omnibus.

Siegfried Sassoon, 22 April 1925

On a bus the other day, a woman with a baby sat opposite, the baby bawled and the woman at once began to unlace herself, exposing a large, red udder, which she swung into the baby's face. The infant, however, continued to cry, and the woman said, 'Come on, there's a good boy – if you don't I shall give it to the gentleman opposite.'

W. N. P. Barbellion, *The Journal of a Disappointed Man* (1920)

Hanging on

With the decline in use of telephone kiosks, BT have sold many of them for £1 to local communities. The uses to which they have been put have been many and various.

Salad bar, in winter with soups and stews
Library
Art gallery
Book exchange
Alehouse
Offices
Shoe-shine bar
Cash machine
Art installation
Mobile-phone repair shop
Tourist information
Colour therapy room
Coffee bar
Cake, pickles and preserves shop
Ice-cream bar
Sandwich bar

In one community a lap-dancing bar was proposed but was turned down in favour of a defibrillator. No doubt to slow the racing heart.

Various news reports

Our debt to Shakespeare

Not slept one wink	*Cymbeline*
With bated breath	*The Merchant of Venice*
Neither here nor there	*Othello*
Seal your lips and give no words but mum	*Henry IV, Part II*
Full circle	*King Lear*
Knock knock! Who's there?	*Macbeth*
Will wear my heart on my sleeve	*Othello*
Send him packing	*Henry VI*
Though this be madness yet there is method in it	*Hamlet*
Wild goose chase	*Romeo and Juliet*
Lie low	*Much Ado about Nothing*
What the dickens	*The Merry Wives of Windsor*
The be all and end all	*Macbeth*
Salad days	*Antony and Cleopatra*
More in sorrow than in anger	*Hamlet*
Into thin air	*The Tempest*
A blinking idiot	*The Merchant of Venice*
It was Greek to me	*Julius Caesar*
Bag and baggage	*As You Like It*
More sinn'd against than sinning	*King Lear*

I'm not absolutely certain of my facts, but I rather fancy it's Shakespeare who says that it's always just when a fellow is feeling particularly braced with things in general that Fate sneaks up behind him with the bit of lead piping.

P. G. Wodehouse, 'Jeeves and the Unbidden Guest' (1919)

News from Suffolk

'The right to trial by combat was introduced to Britain by the Normans in 1066,' Leon Humphreys told the magistrates' court in Bury St Edmunds, 'and I wish my guilt or innocence to be decided by that method. I have been charged with failing to notify the DVLA that my Suzuki 125cc motorcycle was off the road, but it is my property, and my right to do what I like with it. The right to trial by combat is still on the statute books, and I can ask for it because Human Rights legislation gives ordinary people the right to use the law for their own purposes. And as I have opted for trial by combat, I do not need to enter a plea of guilty or not guilty. I am willing to fight a champion put up by the DVLA, but they must remember that this will be a fight to the death. I am prepared to fight with Japanese samurai swords, Gurkha knives, or blacksmith's hammers. According to mediaeval law, the victor speaks in the name of God and justice, so it is a reasonable enough way of sorting the matter out.'

Magistrates rejected Humphreys' request and fined him £200 with £100 costs. A court spokesman later told reporters, 'If this man claims he has the right to trial by combat, then he will have to present the court with evidence of the relevant legislation. The practice was commonplace until the 1300s, when the system of trial by jury or magistrates began to be introduced instead. I am not aware that anyone has the right to trial by combat these days.'

Ipswich Star, 2 November 2002
(thanks to Jim Cox)

Unreliable witnesses

These are from a book called Disorder in the Courts, *compiled by Charles M. Sevilla, and are things people actually said in court in America, taken down by court reporters* verbatim.

ATTORNEY: What gear were you in at the moment of the impact?
WITNESS: Gucci sweats and Reeboks.

ATTORNEY: Are you sexually active?
WITNESS: No, I just lie there.

ATTORNEY: What is your date of birth?
WITNESS: July 18th.
ATTORNEY: What year?
WITNESS: Every year.

ATTORNEY: Can you describe the individual?
WITNESS: He was about medium height and had a beard.
ATTORNEY: Was this a male or a female?
WITNESS: Unless the Circus was in town I'm going with male.

ATTORNEY: Is your appearance here this morning pursuant to a
    deposition notice, which I sent to your attorney?
WITNESS: No, this is how I dress when I go to work.

ATTORNEY: Doctor, how many of your autopsies have you
    performed on dead people?
WITNESS: All of them. The live ones put up too much of a fight.

ATTORNEY: What was the first thing your husband said to you
    that morning?
WITNESS: He said, 'Where am I, Cathy?'
ATTORNEY: And why did that upset you?
WITNESS: My name is Susan!

ATTORNEY: This myasthenia gravis, does it affect your memory at all?
WITNESS: Yes.
ATTORNEY: And in what ways does it affect your memory?
WITNESS: I forget.
ATTORNEY: You forget? Can you give us an example of something you forgot?

ATTORNEY: Now doctor, isn't it true that when a person dies in his sleep, he doesn't know about it until the next morning?
WITNESS: Did you actually pass the bar exam?

ATTORNEY: The youngest son, the 20-year-old, how old is he?
WITNESS: He's 20, much like your IQ.

ATTORNEY: So the date of conception (of the baby) was August 8th?
WITNESS: Yes.
ATTORNEY: And what were you doing at that time?
WITNESS: Getting laid.

ATTORNEY: She had three children, right?
WITNESS: Yes.
ATTORNEY: How many were boys?
WITNESS: None.
ATTORNEY: Were there any girls?
WITNESS: Your Honor, I think I need a different attorney. Can I get a new attorney?

ATTORNEY: How was your first marriage terminated?
WITNESS: By death.
ATTORNEY: And by whose death was it terminated?
WITNESS: Take a guess.

ATTORNEY: ALL your responses MUST be oral, ok? What school did you go to?

WITNESS: Oral . . .

ATTORNEY: Do you recall the time that you examined the body?

WITNESS: The autopsy started around 8.30 p.m.

ATTORNEY: And Mr Denton was dead at the time?

WITNESS: If not, he was by the time I finished.

And last:

ATTORNEY: Doctor, before you performed the autopsy, did you check for a pulse?

WITNESS: No.

ATTORNEY: Did you check for blood pressure?

WITNESS: No.

ATTORNEY: Did you check for breathing?

WITNESS: No.

ATTORNEY: So, then it is possible that the patient was alive when you began the autopsy?

WITNESS: No.

ATTORNEY: How can you be so sure, Doctor?

WITNESS: Because his brain was sitting on my desk in a jar.

ATTORNEY: I see, but could the patient have still been alive, nevertheless?

WITNESS: Yes, it is possible that he could have been alive and practising law.

Thanks to my secretary Rachel

Something for everyone

Some of the more interesting political parties contesting the 2015
General Election:

> Above and Beyond Party
> Beer, Baccy and Scratchings
> Cannabis is Safer than Alcohol
> Common Sense Party
> Keep It Real
> Magna Carta Party
> Monster Raving Loony Party
> No Description
> Pirate Party UK
> Reduce VAT in Sport
> Removing the Politicians
> Something New
> The 30–50 Coalition
> The Birthday Party
> The Eccentric Party of Great Britain
> Vapers in Power
> World Peace through Song

The day before the 2005 General Election

Sir,
Independent single male, late 20s, homeowner, motor enthusiast
and smoker. Likes adventure and the finer things in life; wine,
travel and good food; seeks political party prepared to leave me
alone.

Daniel Cuthbert, Brentwood,
letter to the *Daily Telegraph,* 4 May 2005

Our NHS?

We trained hard but it seems that every time we were beginning to form a team we would be reorganized. I was to learn later in life that we tend to meet any new situation by reorganizing, and a wonderful method it can be for creating the illusion of progress while producing confusion, inefficiency and demoralization.

Titus Petronius, AD 27

Friends divided

Sir William Waller, Parliamentarian commander in the west of England, replies to a request for a personal interview from his old friend and Cavalier opponent Sir Ralph Hopton, in 1643:

The experience I have had of your worth, and the happiness I have enjoyed in your friendship are wounding considerations when I look upon this present distance between us. Certainly my affections to you are so unchangeable, that hostility itself cannot violate my friendship to your person, but I must be true to the cause wherein I serve. The old limitation *usque ad aras* [as far as the altar, i.e. for ever] holds still and where my conscience is interested, all other obligations are swallowed up.

I should gladly wait on you according to your desire, but that I look upon you as you are engaged in that party, beyond a possibility of retreat and consequently uncapable of being wrought upon by any persuasion. And I know the conference could never be so close between us, but that it would take wind and receive a construction to my dishonour. That great God, which is the searcher of my heart, knows with what a sad sense I go upon this service and with what a perfect hatred I detest this war without any enemy. But I look upon it as *opus domini*, which is enough to silence all passion in me.

The God of peace in his good time send us peace and in the meantime fit us to receive it. We are both upon the stage and must act those parts assigned to us in this tragedy. Let us do it in a way of honour and without personal animosities whatsoever the issue be, I shall never willingly relinquish the dear title of your most affectionate friend and faithful servant, William Waller.

S. R. Gardiner, *History of the Great Civil War, 1642–1649* (1886–91)

Definitions

ABSURDITY

A statement of belief manifestly inconsistent with one's own opinion.

EDUCATION

That which discloses to the wise and disguises from the foolish their levels of understanding.

From Ambrose Bierce, The Devil's Dictionary (1911)

Sir,

Ian Cherry's letter reminded me of the time when my MBA class at Imperial College in the mid-1990s debated whether the study of management was an art or a science.

We concluded that it was a foreign language.

Anna Whelan, Orkney,
letter to The Times, 7 August 2012

Musings on passports

Sir,
Some years ago a colleague lost his passport in Paris and was allowed back into the UK on the authority of a Battersea library ticket.

Sir,
When Finchley Cricket Club went on tour to Holland in 1980 one of our party forgot his passport and was allowed to travel freely, there and back, by showing the UK and Dutch officials his name on a label that his mother had sewn into the waistband of his cricket trousers.

Sir,
Arriving for lunch at the Reichstag, we found that passports were required for entry. After five, rather long, minutes we were admitted on the strength of our North-West Leicestershire old-age bus passes.

Sir,
Some years ago a fellow member of my choir forgot his passport but was allowed to travel from Heathrow to Edinburgh on his only form of ID, his choir membership card. The airport official said: 'We don't think a member of the London Gay Men's Choir would be a terrorist.'

From letters to the Daily Telegraph, June 2014

Weather

For some time now I have been surprised and intrigued by some of the terms used by those who present the weather forecast on television. A selection:

Showers draped across the east coast

Usable weather

Rogue showers

Up and down weather

Organized rain

Moody skies in Kent

Showers sprouting up over England

Rain flirting with the east coast

Soft hail

This week we open the door to the Atlantic

Some showers will continue to peck away

Cricketing eccentrics

Jack Russell, Gloucestershire and England

Artists have a reputation for eccentricity, witness Caravaggio's boozy brawls and Salvador Dalí's moustache. The wicket keeper/painter, Russell, is up there with the queerest. Terrier-like in pursuit of perfection, he drove his sponsored car to games wearing a sleeping bag with the bottom cut off, a ruse to keep his back and legs from stiffening up. He also took teabags on tour and would re-use them endlessly, drying them on the end of his bed overnight. A private man, Russell routinely blindfolded visitors to his Gloucestershire home. 'We know where you live,' was a favourite sledge from his opponents.

Harold Bird, Yorkshire and Leicestershire

As a player, Dickie Bird was fretful; as an umpire, away from the moderating influence of the dressing-room, he was plain bonkers. Most of his oddities – like his arrest while climbing into The Oval at 5.30 on the morning of his first-class umpiring debut – stemmed from a morbid fear of being late. Asked to lunch with the Queen ('I set off from Barnsley at 5 a.m., I thought I'd give myself enough time'), he turned up for breakfast and was told to go away.

Wisden Cricketer, September 2005

Bowled over

Following the greatest Ashes series in 2005 (England 2: Australia, 1)
I found this surprisingly pertinent account in the 1954 Wisden:

Australians in England, 1953

Rarely has any series of matches produced such interesting and
exciting cricket. Day after day and sometimes hour after hour
the pendulum swung first towards Australia and then towards
England. Time and again it seemed that one of the teams had
established absolute mastery only for it to be taken away. No
other series of tests captured such public attention. What with
day by day front page newspaper articles and radio and
television broadcasts, there were times when industry almost
stood still, while the man in the street followed the tense battle
between bat and ball.

And in the same year I came across this:

The only tree inside the boundary of a first-class cricket ground
has been blown down by high winds after 158 years as a 'wooden
fielder'.

The lime tree at Kent's ground in Canterbury, south-east
England, deprived generations of players of a six.

'It was a very, very effective fielder,' said Club Curator David
Robertson on Monday. 'We feel shock and sadness really, it was
one of the great traditions of Kent cricket. Shots blocked by the
tree were counted as a four and only three batsmen cleared the
90-foot tree to score a six – Jim Smith of Middlesex in 1939, the
West Indies' Leary Constantine in 1928 and Karl Hooper in 1992.'

Hindu Newspaper, India, 12 January 2005

Speak, memory!

In May 2016, the London Library celebrated its 175th anniversary, hosting a number of events in a marquee in St James's Square. Christine and I attended one relating to Cricket and Writing with thoughts and comments from a panel which included Mike Brearley, Mike Atherton, Tim Rice, Ramachandra Guha and Emma John. Questions were invited. One was from an elderly silver-haired gentleman in the front row, who prefaced his question by saying that as soon as it was answered he would have to leave: he had to get back to the West Country because he was playing in a match the following day and he was 85 years old.

He was thanked for his question and, as he rose to leave, Mike Atherton asked him which team he was playing against.

'I can't remember,' he replied.

As you grow old, you lose interest in sex, your friends drift away, your children often ignore you. There are many other advantages of course, but these would seem to be the outstanding ones.

Richard Nerdham, *Toronto Globe and Mail*,
from John Julius Norwich's *Christmas Cracker*, 2004

Guests

'Welcome the coming, speed the parting guest.'

Odyssey, Book XV, line 74

This was used as a quotation by the ancients, as well as by the modern world. Perhaps Shakespeare caught its echo when he wrote in *Troilus and Cressida*:

> For time is like a fashionable host
> That slightly shakes his parting guest by th'hand,
> And with his arms outstretch'd, as he would fly,
> Grasps in the comer; welcome ever smiles
> And farewell goes out sighing.

From Maurice Baring's *Have You Anything to Declare?* (1936)

I am reminded of the time Christine and I were the guests of honour at a medical dinner in Dhaka, Bangladesh, and had enjoyed a pleasant meal and company. When the meal ended there was considerable uncertainty in the air, even after people had left the table. It wasn't clear what was coming next. And then, very quietly, one of the organizers of the dinner came up to us and said politely, 'We are waiting for you to leave.'

During our travels in Italy in the summer of 2006, we came across this notice in the reception foyer of the Villa Barone hotel in Tuscany:

'All guests make us happy – some by coming, others by leaving.'

Overdue linguistic reform

The European Commission has just announced an agreement whereby English will be the official language of the European Union rather than German, which was the other possibility.

As part of the negotiations, the British Government conceded that English spelling had some room for improvement and has accepted a 5-year phase-in plan that would become known as 'Euro-English'.

In the first year, 's' will replace the soft 'c'. Sertainly, this will make the sivil servants jump with joy. The hard 'c' will be dropped in favour of 'k'. This should clear up konfusion, and keyboards kan have one less letter.

There will be growing public enthusiasm in the second year when the troublesome 'ph' will be replaced with 'f'. This will make words like fotograf 20% shorter.

In the 3rd year, public akseptanse of the new spelling kan be expected to reach the stage where more komplikated changes are possible.

Governments will encourage the removal of double letters which have always ben a deterent to akurate speling.

Also, al wil agre that the horibl mes of the silent 'e' in the language is disgrasful and it should go away.

By the 4th yer, people will be reseptiv to steps such as replasing 'th' with 'z' and 'w' with 'v'.

During ze fifz yer, ze unesesary 'o' can be dropd from vords containing 'ou' and after ziz fifz yer, ve vil hav a reil sensibl riten styl.

Zer vil be no mor trubl or difikultis and evrivun vil find it ezi tu understand ech oza. Ze drem of a united urop vil finali kum tru.

Und efter ze fifz yer, ve vil al be speking German like zey vunted in ze forst plas.

Brussels Journal, 25 October 2006
(thanks to Brian Dunn)

On the value of summit meetings

'Mrs Thatcher did not like them. There were foreigners present and too many people discussing compromises.'

Jonathan Powell on BBC Radio 4

An urban myth?

Outside Bristol Zoo there is a car park for 150 cars and 8 buses.

For 25 years the parking fees were managed by a very pleasant car park attendant.

The fees were £1.40 for cars and about £7 for buses.

Then, one day, after 25 solid years of never missing a day off work, the car parking attendant just didn't show up; so Zoo Management called the City Council and asked them to send another car parking attendant.

The Council did some research and replied that the car park was the Zoo's responsibility.

The Zoo advised the Council that the car parking attendant was a City employee.

The City Council responded that the attendant had never been on the City payroll.

Meanwhile, sitting in his villa somewhere on the coast of Spain or France or Italy . . . is a man who'd apparently had a ticket machine installed completely on his own, and then had simply begun to show up every day to collect and keep the parking fees, estimated at about £560 per day – for 25 years.

Assuming 7 days a week, this amounts to just over £7 million . . . and no one even knows his name.

Bristol Post, 15 June 2009
(thanks to my secretary Rachel)

Modern life

After the economic crash of 2008 a cartoon appeared in Private Eye
with this caption:

> The triumph of Capitalism
> 'No one emerges with any credit.'

19 September 2008

Strike at Californian walnut processing factory called off after
13 years.

Independent on Sunday, 10 April 2005

An oasis of civilization in a desert of democracy

The description of the oldest gentleman's club in London,
White's, founded in 1693, by its historian Percy Coulson

The coast: Norfolk

As on the highway's quiet edge
He mows the grass beside the hedge,
The old man has for company
The distant, grey, salt-smelling sea,
A poppied field, a cow and calf,
The finches on the telegraph.

Across his faded back, a hone,
He slowly, slowly scythes alone,
In silence of the wind-soft air,
With ladies' bedstraw everywhere,
With whitened corn, and tarry poles,
And far-off gulls like risen souls.

Frances Cornford, 1948

Fertile ground

Email from Philip to Jim Cox:

Chris is well, we have recently been able to add two small neighbours' gardens to ours (i.e. gardens, not neighbours) so she has been hard at work with new planting etc and further grandchildren keep appearing.

Reply from Jim to Philip:

. . . Please advise Chris that creating grandchildren through horticulture is an ingenious project with huge potential but it may fall foul of Human Fertilization and Embryology Authority guidelines. I hope that when we meet in September, you will tell us more about the techniques involved and the underlying scientific theory.

The Queen to Alan Titchmarsh, gardening expert:

'You have given a lot of women a lot of pleasure.'

Independent on Sunday, 18 August 2002

Edna O'Brien was the first Irish woman to have sex. For some decades she was the only Irish woman to have had sex – the rest just had children.

Anne Enright, reviewing O'Brien's *The Light of Evening*
in the *Guardian*, 14 October 2006

Vive la différence

The building of the Channel Tunnel necessitated no fewer than a dozen immense drills, six on each side. The English machines were numbered from one to six; the French, on the other hand, were named Brigitte, Europa, Catherine, Virginie, Pascoline and Séverine.

John Julius Norwich's Christmas Cracker, 2015

A bilingual sign spotted in a DIY supermarket in France:

'Quincaillerie. Hardware. Ornamental screwing'

Simon Hoggart, Guardian, 22 October 2011

'Whilst in Normandy last summer, I found Bisto gravy powder in a hardware shop on the same shelf as colouring for tile grout.'

M. J. Tanner

We were discussing the possibility of making one of our cats Pope recently, and we decided that the fact that she was not Italian and was female, made the third point, that she was a cat, quite irrelevant.

Katherine Whitehorn

Travels

I am grateful to Dick Soper for sending me this extract from the menu of the Alhambra Palace in Granada, Spain:

All desserts are elaborated at the moment of commandment.

And more of notices in hotels abroad. My secretary Rachel has introduced me to Lost in Translation *by Charlie Croker*

An extract from Finland:

If you cannot reach a fire exit, close the door and expose yourself at the window.

And one from Austria:

Not to perambulate in the hours of repose in the boots of ascension.

Greekonomics

It is a slow day in a little Greek village. The rain is beating down and the streets are deserted. Times are tough, everybody is in debt, and everybody lives on credit.

On this particular day a rich German tourist is driving through the village. He stops at the local hotel and lays a €100 note on the desk, telling the hotel owner he wants to inspect the rooms upstairs in order to pick one to spend the night.

The owner gives him some keys and, as soon as the visitor has walked upstairs, the hotelier grabs the €100 note and runs next door to pay his debt to the butcher.

The butcher takes the €100 note and runs down the street to repay his debt to the pig farmer. The pig farmer takes the €100 note and heads off to pay his bill at the supplier of feed and fuel.

The guy at the Farmers' Co-op takes the €100 note and runs to pay his drinks bill at the taverna.

The taverna owner slips the money along to the local prostitute drinking at the bar, who has also been facing hard times and has had to offer him 'services' on credit.

The hooker then rushes to the hotel and pays off her room bill to the hotel owner with the €100 note.

The hotel proprietor then places the €100 note back on the counter so the rich traveller will not suspect anything. At that moment the traveller comes down the stairs, picks up the €100 note, states that the rooms are not satisfactory, pockets the money, and leaves town.

No one produced anything. No one earned anything. However, the whole village is now out of debt and looking to the future with a lot more optimism. And that, Ladies and Gentlemen, is how the bailout package works.

2008
Thanks to Scott Brown

Retirement

When Christine retired, she was delighted to come across this passage in a letter Charles Lamb wrote to William Wordsworth on retiring from the East India Company after thirty-three years:

I came home for EVER on Tuesday in last week. The incomprehensibleness of my condition overwhelmed me. It was like passing from life into eternity. Every year to be as long as three, i.e. to have three times as much real time, time that is my own, in it! I wandered about thinking I was happy, but feeling I was not. But that tumultuousness is passing off, and I begin to understand the nature of the gift. Holidays, even the annual month, were always uneasy joys; their conscious fugitiveness – the craving after making the most of them. Now, when all is holiday, there are no holidays. I can sit at home, in rain or shine, without a restless impulse for walkings. I am daily steadying, and shall soon find it as natural to me to be my own master, as it has been irksome to have a master.

6 April 1825

Arm-waving

Even as a conductor Barenboim says that he can still learn more. If one of his ideas doesn't work he says he's happy to try something else. This contrasts with the tantrums thrown by the previous generation of maestros, such as his predecessor at the Chicago Symphony Orchestra, Sir Georg Solti. 'You can't put this in,' says Barenboim, 'but Solti could be very direct and his English was colourful sometimes. Once he said to an orchestra' – Barenboim imitates Solti's strident pitched Hungarian tones – 'You think I know fuck-nothing. I know fuck-all!'

Interview with Daniel Barenboim by Sholto Byrnes,
Independent on Sunday, 8 January 2006

To testiculate:

To wave your arms around when speaking and talking complete bollocks.

The appropriately named Ed Balls detailing the Prime Minister's agenda:

'The priority for him is that the country knows that his priority is delivering on their priorities.'

Guardian, 29 September 2007

'The Green Belt is a Labour achievement and we intend to build on it.'

John Prescott, 1998

When insults had class

These glorious insults are from an era before the English language was boiled down to four-letter words:

A Member of Parliament to Disraeli: 'Sir, you will either die on the gallows or of some unspeakable disease.'

'That depends, Sir,' said Disraeli, 'whether I embrace your policies or your mistress.'

'I have never killed a man, but I have read many obituaries with great pleasure.'

Clarence Darrow

'Thank you for sending me a copy of your book; I'll waste no time reading it.'

Moses Hadas

'He has no enemies, but is intensely disliked by his friends . . .'

Oscar Wilde

'I am enclosing two tickets to the first night of my new play; bring a friend, if you have one.'

George Bernard Shaw to Winston Churchill

'Cannot possibly attend first night; will attend second, if there is one.'

Winston Churchill to George Bernard Shaw
(thanks to my stepson Karl)

Party politics

The arrival in the past few days of a handful of different birthday invitations got me thinking about the various stages of life as expressed through party planning.

21st: In your twenties, life is pretty much one big party. We are talking loud music, nasty toilets, thick smoke, cheap booze and the search for sex. Venue: I don't know – it was somewhere near Tufnell Park.

30th: Much like the earlier parties but with garlic bread. The booze is a little better, the bar more salubrious and the party no longer reliant on parents being out of town. While still essentially committed to sex, drugs and rock 'n' roll, people tend to leave with the person with whom they arrived. Guests expect food. A maximum of two jazz tracks is permitted to show your refined taste, but only early on. Those making real money may opt for a jaunt abroad with five mates. Venue: wine bars, nightclubs, the flat you share with three mates, Estonia.

40th: The 'I've still got it' party. Some will be prepared to settle for a nice dinner. Forty is the age at which we need to prove that though we may be stressed parents, weighted down with bags under our eyes and post-baby bellies (especially the men), we can still party. This is the night where you rave right up till 11, when you have to be home for the babysitter. The drink still flows but it is a nice white wine, and the only drugs in sight are Nurofen and antihistamines.

The typical 40th birthday party is characterized by a large rented room with a disco far too loud to allow any sensible conversation, and a 1980s theme – bad wigs, loud colours, a general bad-taste explosion. Or maybe a 1970s theme – bad wigs, loud colours, a general bad-taste explosion. This is because, hey, we're still fun and an essential part of still being fun is showing we don't take ourselves so seriously that we are no longer prepared to look like a pillock.

Fancy dress does present a problem, however, for those who are, in fact, not still fun and not young at heart. My last invitation to a 1980s night was something of a challenge. I considered going as the National Dock Labour Scheme but was badly let down by the local fancy dress shops. In the end, I wore a suit and told everyone I had come as Norman Fowler, although when you do that, you spend the night worrying about bumping into someone with the same outfit. Venue: your house, a tennis or rowing club, a trendy restaurant, a gastro-pub.

50th: In contrast with the desperately-clinging-on-to-youth 40th birthday, the 50th is a statement party. This is likely to be as good as it gets in terms of wealth, health and position, although if you want a statement party, it may be safer to have your 50th at 45. This is a tasteful party with a bit of fun. It will either be held at your palatial home or at a swanky rented location. There will be a disco, or maybe even a live band, but the music will not be too intrusive until the designated dance hour. The food will be high quality, there will be speeches and you will invite the most important people you know. Venue: your London home as long as there is room for a marquee, a country hotel, the Chiltern Firehouse, the Natural History Museum, your weekend retreat in Provence.

60th: A bit of a downer, so you may give it a miss unless you decide to hold a 'free bus pass' party to show off your still-impish sense of humour. Those who do are determined to show they are as young as they were at 40. So 40th birthday rules apply, but the music is a lot quieter and some of the bad wigs are for real.

70th: Thrown by your children because they fear you will not make it to 75. Venue: one of your children's houses. No music. Catered. Over by 10.30 p.m.

80th: Thrown by your grandchildren because, yay, you're still here. Venue: Somewhere with an armchair.

90th: Very much like the 80th, but now your children need armchairs too.

100th: Something fairly last minute. We didn't want to waste the deposit.

Robert Shrimsley, Financial Times, 19 February 2016

A wine-loving lady called Clare
Said whenever she had an affair
'Give me Latour or Lafite
And I'll love you a treat
But I'm no good on *vin ordinaire*.'

Ray Bowden,
past Chairman of The Wine Society

Facing the music

Sir,
On leaving the crematorium (after my funeral) I should like the jolly march 'Blaze Away' played by André Rieu. My husband never listens to a word I say, but he reads the letters in *The Times* very carefully.

Sir,
My mother wanted 'Smoke Gets in Your Eyes' at her cremation. She still had a sense of humour even at the age of 107 when she died.

Sir,
I well remember as a choir girl singing at the wedding of a bride who was very heavily pregnant. The first hymn chosen was 'Dear Lord and Father of Mankind, Forgive Our Foolish Ways'.

Sir,
A former vicar of this parish told me that having conducted a cremation service for a butcher, mourners departed to Bach's 'Sheep May Safely Graze'.

Sir,
A group of us from our local male choir are sometimes engaged to sing at the local crematorium. We are known informally as the Cremtones.

Sir,
I was told by a very old Evangelical Christian of my acquaintance that a revivalist meeting was held in the North of England to which the mayor and corporation were invited. As they had not appeared at the appointed hour, it was decided that the congregation should launch into the opening hymn; whereupon the dignitaries, led by the mayor, duly appeared and processed up the aisle to the sound of several hundred lusty voices singing 'See the Mighty Hosts Advancing, Satan at Their Head'.

Letters to *The Times*, April 2014

Show us a sign

The Revd Ian Gregory forwarded me a letter from a former member of his flock in Glasgow whose friend keeps failing her driving test. So frequently has she failed that people now turn up to watch when another test is due. After her latest failure, someone asked the examiner what went wrong. 'I asked her to tell me a road sign she might see when driving in the country,' he said. 'She replied, "Pick your own strawberries."'

The Times, 3 August 2015

Sign seen at the Dubai Cricket Stadium, Pakistan v England, 2nd Test Match, 17 January 2012

The Dress Code is very simple,
Just keep your clothes on.

I have always been encouraged by the car park machine at the John Radcliffe Hospital in Oxford, advising, 'Change is possible'.

Letter to the *Guardian*, 24 April 2015

Town and country

One old friend to another, 'They're taking them out of our pen now, Jim.'

Overheard at a country funeral, Spring 2004

Sunday Lunch, from a field near here

Seen on a board outside the Saracen's Head
in the isolated Norfolk village of Wolterton

Last week a friend of mine was stopped and questioned by police in Whitehall. He aroused their suspicions, they told him, because he was wearing Wellington boots.

Charles Moore, *Spectator*, 12 March 2005

Peter Lilley's wife tried to get into a Downing Street function saying, 'I'm one of the ministers' wives!' The policeman: 'I couldn't let you in if you were the minister's only wife.'

Simon Carr, *Independent*, 26 May 2010

Local heroes

On the Australian floods in 2011:

Yet from unimaginable scenes of death and destruction have emerged a million good news stories. Of the heroes such as Ken Otto, 62, who saved his parents Fred, 86, and Veen, 84, when the floods came to Grantham, by strapping them in lifejackets and tethering them to a backyard shed.

Sydney Morning Herald, 15 January 2011
(thanks to my stepson Mark Winter)

Country juries are wonderful and they know more about their neighbours than judges, barristers and policemen give them credit for.

The classic story of a jury was at Dubbo (New South Wales) where a man was on trial for stealing some heifers. When the jury returned with their verdict, they were asked, 'Do you find the accused guilty or not guilty of cattle stealing?'

To which the foreman replied 'Not guilty, if he returns the cows.'

The judge read the jury the riot act and concluded by saying, 'Go out and reconsider your verdict and find a true verdict according to the evidence.'

The jury retired again, and when they returned had a belligerent air about them.

They were asked, 'Have you decided on your verdict?'

The foreman said, 'Yes we have. We find the accused not guilty – and he doesn't have to return the cows.'

A. S. Gillespie-Jones, *The Lawyer Who Laughed* (1982)

From the American papers

Federal agents raid gun shop, find weapons

Get 50% off or half price, whichever is less

Statistics show that teen pregnancy drops off significantly after age 25

Alton attorney accidentally sues himself

County to pay $250,000 to advertise lack of funds

Wanted: somebody to go back in time with me. This is not a joke. PO Box 322, Oakview, CA 93022. You'll get paid after we get back. Must bring your own weapons. Safety not guaranteed. I have only done this once before

1995 Nissan Maxima, green, leather, loaded CD, auto start, sunroof, 4-door, good condition, $4,500. Not for sale

Thanks to my brother Robert

Mirror, mirror

Fleet Street isn't what it was. Mike Molloy, who edited the *Daily Mirror* in the 1970s and 1980s, has just published an entertaining memoir called *The Happy Hack*. He had quite a motley crew working for him. When Molloy took over, the *Mirror* had a motoring correspondent who was banned from driving after failing a breath test, a gardening correspondent who only owned a window box, a slimming correspondent who was perpetually a stone and a half overweight and a travel editor who was banned from flying with British Airways after a bout of cabin rage.

'There was also a delightful feature writer who hadn't written an article in five years,' Molloy says. 'Six years later we gave him a farewell dinner at the Ritz Hotel – and he still hadn't written anything.'

The Times, Diary, 2 April 2016

A retired policeman advised that a local newspaper once described a colleague as a 'defective inspector'. After a vehement complaint, the newspaper printed a correction, which ended: 'We extend our apologies to him and the rest of the local police farce.'

The Times, Diary, 27 July 2016

There'll always be an England (4)

The sermon this morning: 'Jesus Walks on the Water'. The sermon tonight: 'Searching for Jesus'.

Remember in prayer the many who are sick of our community. Smile at someone who is hard to love. Say 'Hell' to someone who doesn't care much about you.

Miss Charlene Mason sang 'I will not pass this way again', giving obvious pleasure to the congregation.

The Associate Minister unveiled the church's new campaign slogan last Sunday: 'I Upped My Pledge – Up Yours.'

Thanks to my secretary Rachel

My favourite comment on the birth of Prince George in 2013 to the Duke and Duchess of Cambridge was the headline in Private Eye:

'WOMAN HAS BABY'

With the birth of his sister, perhaps this journalistic high point was surpassed by the Royal Correspondent of the BBC News Channel who said:

'The Duchess of Cambridge is believed to have been present at the birth.'

Al hayle Bertkin

Readers of my Commonplace selections will be aware of my enjoyment of P. G. Wodehouse. You can imagine my pleasure on coming across the following:

My single most deranged possession has to be a six-volume set entirely devoted to translations of one Wodehouse short story, 'The Great Sermon Handicap'. It is offered in 58 different languages and dialects, ranging from Coptic and Icelandic ('Gamli, Godi, Bertie!, Sagdi, Claude') to Basque, French Creole, Somali, Latin ('Bingo, Jaevio, Enim'Inqit, Animus, Aleandi, Non Inest'), Sanskrit, Yiddish, Middle High German and, with complete assurance, Chaucerian English: 'Al hayl Bertkin, he answerede with drery and distract visage.'

Anthony Lane, The New Yorker, 19 April 2004

Sir,
As I was going to sleep, Himself read me Wodehouse's own description of the Empress feeding: 'A sort of gulpy, gurgly, plobby, squishy, wofflesome sound, like a thousand eager men drinking soup in a foreign restaurant'.
    Twenty words are worth a thousand pictures.

Letter to the Daily Telegraph, 17 January 2013
(thanks to my secretary Rachel)

Words, words, words

Ibn Battutah, whose name translates variously as Son of a
Duck, Egg-shaped Bottle and Bad Woman with Ellipsoidal
Body . . .

From The Travels of Ibn Battutah, ed. Tim Mackintosh-Smith

Your report of the discovery of a first edition of *The Importance
of Being Ernest* ('Wilde generosity gives Oxfam shop a £650
boost') omits the highly relevant fact that it was found in a
handbag.

Robert Hill, Leeds, letter to the Guardian, 25 October 2007

Regarding a phrase in our obituary of Dick Francis, a reader
writes: 'The concept of an unauthorized autobiography is an
interesting one!'

Guardian, 17 February 2010

Ough, more oughs

Sir,
In the quote 'the rough-coated, dough-faced ploughman
wandered thoughtfully, coughing and hiccoughing through the
streets of Scarborough on his way to the loughs of Ireland',
we have 'ough' in nine different renditions.

Letter to the Independent, 24 November 2004

Political spin

It all depends on how you look at things . . . Judy Wallman, a professional genealogy researcher in southern California, was doing some personal work on her own family tree. She discovered that Congressman Harry Reid's great-great-uncle, Remus Reid, was hanged for horse stealing and train robbery in Montana in 1889. Both Judy and Congressman Harry Reid share this common ancestor.

The only known photograph of Remus shows him standing on the gallows in Montana territory. On the back of the picture Judy obtained during her research is this inscription: 'Remus Reid, horse thief, sent to Montana Territorial Prison 1885, escaped 1887, robbed the Montana Flyer six times. Caught by Pinkerton detectives, convicted and hanged in 1889.'

So Judy recently emailed Congressman Harry Reid for information about their mutual great-great-uncle.

Harry Reid's staff sent back the following biographical sketch for her genealogy research: 'Remus Reid was a famous cowboy in the Montana Territory. His business empire grew to include acquisition of valuable equestrian assets and intimate dealings with the Montana railroad. Beginning in 1883, he devoted several years of his life to government service, finally taking leave to resume his dealings with the railroad. In 1887, he was a key player in a vital investigation run by the renowned Pinkerton Detective Agency. In 1889 Remus passed away during an important civic function held in his honour when the platform upon which he was standing collapsed.'

Thanks to my stepson Karl

The Royal Navy

'I wish Nelson would stop signalling. We all know well enough what to do.'

Admiral Collingwood, Trafalgar, 21 October 1805

Mr Houghton, shoemaker, in the Buttermarket in Bury St Edmunds. He was in apparent good health, chopping a faggot, the same afternoon, when he accidentally cut off one of his fingers, and on his wife expressing a wish to dress it, he said, 'Never mind, my dear; what is this wound compared to Lord Nelson's?' And immediately fell down in an apoplectic fit, from which he never recovered to answer another sentence.

The Gentlemen's Magazine, 1806

In correspondence it had been suggested that HMS Victory *would benefit by being sheltered from the weather under cover.*

Sir,
I can see the logic. Might I suggest a bottle?

Letter to The Times, 4 February 2014

Admiralty Stores List, Second World War

> Pots, Chamber, plain
> Pots, Chamber, with Admiralty monogram in blue, for hospital use
> Pots, Chamber, fluted, with royal cipher in gold, for flag officers only
> Pots, Chamber, round, rubber, lunatic

New Statesman, 29 November 1999

Modes of address

Sir,
Even in the 1970s my father, a field marshal, was frequently addressed as Dear Mr Marshall, and, even more intimately, as Dear Field.

Rupert Baker, Grateley,
letter to *The Times*, January 2014

Sir,
My mother (maiden name Captain) served as a sergeant in a division of the British Army in India during the war. So she was Sergeant Captain. In the same division was a Captain Sergeant. There was even a rumour they had a soft spot for each other. Fortunately she married someone with a far more sensible and pronounceable surname.

Rutton Viccajee, Guildford
letter to *The Times*, January 2014

The ideal guest

Question: Who would you most like to sit next to at a dinner party?

Answer: Someone who knows the difference between conversation and monologue.

Small Talk with Barry Unsworth,
Financial Times, 18 December 2009

God Save the Queen!

In 2016 Marc and Karen Rivo of Miami Beach, Florida, sent me the following letter, addressed to the citizens of the United States of America from Her Sovereign Majesty Queen Elizabeth II:

In the light of your failure to nominate competent candidates for President of the USA and thus govern yourselves, we hereby give notice of the revocation of your independence, effective immediately.

Her Sovereign Majesty Queen Elizabeth II will resume monarchical duties over all states, commonwealths and territories (except North Dakota, which she does not fancy). Your new Prime Minister, Theresa May, will appoint a Governor for America without need of further elections. The Senate and House of Representatives will be abolished, a questionnaire will be circulated next year to determine whether any of you noticed.

To aid the transition to a British Crown Dependency, the following are introduced with immediate effect.

1. The letter 'u' will be reinstated in words such as colour, favour, labour and neighbour. Likewise you will learn to spell doughnut without skipping half the letters. The word aluminium will be pronounced correctly.
2. Using the same 27 words interspersed with filler noises such as 'like' and 'you know' is an unacceptable and inefficient means of communication. There is no such thing as US English. We will let Microsoft know on your behalf.
3. July 4th will no longer be celebrated.
4. You will learn to resolve personal issues without recourse to guns, lawyers and therapists. The fact that you need so many lawyers and therapists shows that you are not quite ready to be independent. Guns should only be used for shooting pheasant, partridge and grouse. If you can't sort things out without suing someone or speaking to a therapist then you are not ready to shoot grouse.

5. All road intersections will replaced with roundabouts and you will drive on the left side of the road.

6. The former USA will adopt UK prices for petrol (not gasoline).

7. You will learn to make real chips. Those things you call French fries are chips, and those you insist on calling potato chips are properly called crisps.

8. The cold tasteless stuff you insist on calling beer is not actually beer at all. Henceforth, only proper British bitter will be referred to as beer, and European beers of known and accepted provenance will be referred to as lager. American brands will be referred to as Near Frozen Gnat's Urine, so that all can be sold without risk of confusion.

9. Hollywood will be required occasionally to cast English actors as good guys. Hollywood will also be required to cast English actors to play English characters. The portrayal of Mr Bennet in *Pride and Prejudice* by Donald Sutherland is too painful to recall.

10. You will cease playing American Football. There is only one kind of proper football: you call it Soccer. You will be allowed to play Rugby as this does not involve stopping for a rest every 20 seconds or wearing full Kevlar body armour.

11. You will also have to stop playing baseball. It is unreasonable to host an event called the World Series for a game which is not played outside the USA. Since only 2.1% of you are aware that there is a world beyond your borders, your error is understandable. You will play Cricket.

12. You must tell us who killed JFK, it has been driving us mad.

13. Her Majesty's Revenue and Customs will be in touch shortly to ensure the payment of all monies due, backdated to 1776. (This includes you, Mr Trump.)

14. Tea time is at 4 p.m. each afternoon with proper cups and saucers, no mugs, with biscuits (not cookies), cakes, scones, strawberries and cream.

Parson's pleasures

It was an intense frost. I sat down in my bath upon a sheet of
thick ice which broke in the middle into large pieces whilst
sharp points and jagged edges stuck all round the sides of the
tub like *chevaux de frise*, not particularly comforting to the
naked thighs and loins, for the keen ice cut like broken glass.
The ice water stung and scorched like fire. I had to collect the
floating pieces of ice and pile them on a chair before I could use
the sponge and then I had to thaw the sponge in my hands for
it was a mass of ice. The morning was most brilliant . . . the
road sparkled with millions of rainbows, the seven colours
gleaming in every glittering point of hoar frost. The church was
very cold in spite of two roaring stove fires.

Francis Kilvert, *Diary*, Christmas Day 1870

I dined at the Chaplin's table upon roasted tongue and udder.
NB, I shall not dine on roasted tongue and udder again very
soon.

Reverend James Woodforde, *Diary*, 17 February 1763

Acknowledgements

The author and publisher would like to thank the following for permission to reproduce copyright material: p.10, *Observer*; p.11, *GP* magazine; p. 12, © The Estate of Robert Frost; p.13, Emo Philips; p.14, *The Times*; p.15, *Observer*; p.18, *London Review of Books*; p.19, *Guardian*; p.21, *Independent* and *Financial Times*; p.24, *Independent on Sunday*; p. 27, *Independent on Sunday*; p.29, Matt Harvey, 'Water Cooler Moments', *Guardian* and *Where Earwigs Dare*, Green Books, 2010; p.30, Paul Scott, *The Jewel in the Crown*, Random House, 1966; p.31, Tom Stoppard, *Dirty Linen & New-Found-Land*, Faber & Faber, 1976, and Hugh Brogan, *The Penguin History of the USA*, Penguin, 1985; p.32, *Guardian*; p. 33, Alan Bennett, *Writing Home*, Faber & Faber, 1994; p. 35, HMRC; p. 37, *Independent on Sunday*; p. 39, *Washington Post*; p.41, *Guardian*; p.43, *Guardian* and *Country Life*; p. 44, Roger Rosenblatt, *Bibliomania*; p.46, *Guardian*; p.48, *The Times* and Alan Bennett, *Untold Stories*, Profile Books and Faber & Faber, 2006; p.50, *Observer*, *Guardian* and *Private Eye* magazine, by kind permission of, www.private-eye.co.uk; p.53, *Financial Times*; p. 58, Anthony Lane, *The New Yorker*; p.60, *Guardian*; p. 62, © The Estate of Siegfried Sassoon; p.65, 'Jeeves and the Unbidden Guest' from *My Man Jeeves* by P. G. Wodehouse, published by George Newnes, 1919, copyright © P. G. Wodehouse, reproduced by permission of the estate of the author c/o Rogers, Coleridge & White Ltd., 20 Powis Mews, London W11 1JN; p. 66, *Ipswich Star*; p.67, Charles M. Sevilla, *Disorder in the Court*, W. W. Norton, 1999; p.76, *Wisden Cricketer* and p.77, *Wisden Cricketers' Almanack 1954*, reproduced by kind permission of John Wisden & Co Ltd; p. 80, *Brussels Journal*; p. 82, *Bristol Post*; p. 83, *Independent on Sunday*; p.84, reproduced with the permission of the trustees of the Frances Crofts Cornford Will Trust; p.85, *Independent on Sunday* and *Guardian*; p.86, *Guardian*; p. 87, Charlie Croker, *Lost in Translation*, Michael O'Mara Books, 2007; p. 90, *Independent on Sunday* and *Guardian*; p.92, *Financial Times*; p.96, *The Times*; p.97, *Spectator* and *Independent*; p. 98, A. S. Gillespie, *The Lawyer Who Laughed*, Hutchinson, 1982; p. 100, *The Times*; p. 102, Anthony Lane, *The New Yorker*; p.103, *Guardian*; p.107, *Financial Times*.

Every effort has been made to trace the holders of copyright material but in the event that we have failed to do so we would be pleased to hear from them. Please contact Slightly Foxed, 53 Hoxton Square, London N1 6PB.